I0413303

Documenting the Stages and Streamflows Associated With the 2011 Activation of the New Madrid Floodway, Missouri

By Todd A. Koenig and Robert R. Holmes, Jr.

Chapter E of
2011 Floods of the Central United States

Prepared in cooperation with the U.S. Army Corps of Engineers

Professional Paper 1798–E

U.S. Department of the Interior
U.S. Geological Survey

U.S. Department of the Interior
SALLY JEWELL, Secretary

U.S. Geological Survey
Suzette M. Kimball, Acting Director

U.S. Geological Survey, Reston, Virginia: 2013

For more information on the USGS—the Federal source for science about the Earth, its natural and living resources, natural hazards, and the environment, visit http://www.usgs.gov or call 1–888–ASK–USGS.

For an overview of USGS information products, including maps, imagery, and publications, visit http://www.usgs.gov/pubprod

To order this and other USGS information products, visit http://store.usgs.gov

Contents

Figures

Tables

Conversion Factors

Inch/Pound to SI

Multiply	By	To obtain
Length		
inch (in.)	2.54	centimeter (cm)
inch (in.)	25.4	millimeter (mm)
foot (ft)	0.3048	meter (m)
mile (mi)	1.609	kilometer (km)
Area		
acre	4,047	square meter (m^2)
acre	0.004047	square kilometer (km^2)
Volume		
cubic foot (ft^3)	0.02832	cubic meter (m^3)
Flow rate		
foot per second (ft/s)	0.3048	meter per second (m/s)
cubic foot per second (ft^3/s)	0.02832	cubic meter per second (m^3/s)
Pressure		
pound per square inch (lb/in^2)	6.895	kilopascal (kPa)

SI to Inch/Pound

Multiply	By	To obtain
Length		
centimeter (cm)	0.3937	inch (in.)
millimeter (mm)	0.03937	inch (in.)
meter (m)	3.281	foot (ft)
kilometer (km)	0.6214	mile (mi)
Area		
square meter (m^2)	0.0002471	acre
square kilometer (km^2)	247.1	acre
Volume		
cubic meter (m^3)	35.31	cubic foot (ft^3)
Flow rate		
meter per second (m/s)	3.281	foot per second (ft/s)
cubic meter per second (m^3/s)	35.31	cubic foot per second (ft^3/s)
Pressure		
kilopascal (kPa)	0.1450	pound per square inch (lb/in^2)

Vertical coordinate information is referenced to the North American Vertical Datum of 1988 (NAVD 88).

Horizontal coordinate information is referenced to the North American Datum of 1983 (NAD 83).

Altitude, as used in this report, refers to distance above the vertical datum.

Concentrations of chemical constituents in water are given either in milligrams per liter (mg/L) or micrograms per liter (µg/L).

Documenting the Stages and Streamflows Associated With the 2011 Activation of the New Madrid Floodway, Missouri

By Todd A. Koenig and Robert R. Holmes, Jr.

Abstract

The U.S. Geological Survey initiated a substantial effort in the summer of 2011 to measure and document the record-setting floods of the Mississippi and Ohio Rivers, including the reach in and near the New Madrid Floodway. The activation of the floodway, which had not occurred since 1937, provided a rare opportunity to collect a unique dataset describing a flood wave downstream from a levee breach as well as the flow through a large floodway. A total of 42 submersible pressure transducers collected time series of water levels while crews collected hundreds of depth, velocity, and streamflow measurements at selected locations in and near the floodway throughout the period from late April to late June. These data are presented in this chapter.

Introduction

In the spring and summer of 2011, concurrent floods developed in the two primary subbasins of the Mississippi River: the Ohio River and the upper Mississippi River (defined here as the part of the Mississippi River above the confluence with the Ohio River). As the separate flood waves traveled toward their confluence in April 2011, the U.S. Geological Survey (USGS) was alerted to the possibility that the New Madrid Floodway (hereafter referred to as "the floodway"), shown in figure 1, might be activated for the first time since 1937 (Mississippi River Commission, 2012).

The floodway, which is often called the Bird's Point-New Madrid Floodway in U.S. Army Corps of Engineers (USACE) literature, occupies 133,000 acres along the right (west) bank of the Mississippi River immediately below its confluence with the Ohio River (confluence area). The initial floodway construction was completed in October 1932 (Camillo, 2012, p. 42) as part of the larger Mississippi Rivers and Tributaries Project (MR&T), administered by the Mississippi River Commission under the supervision of the USACE. The floodway has been a source of considerable controversy since the Flood Control Act of 1928 authorized the MR&T in the aftermath of the devastating 1927 flood in the Mississippi River Basin (Mississippi River Commission, 2011). The USACE is authorized to operate the floodway to reduce river elevations, upstream from and adjacent to the floodway, that threaten areas such as Cairo, Ill. and the 2.5 million acres (fig. 2) stretching from Commerce, Missouri to just upstream from Helena, Arkansas (Mississippi River Commission, 2011).

Activation of the floodway intentionally floods over 133,000 acres of Missouri farm land. In 2011, it displaced 230 people (Camillo, 2012, p. 87) and flooded their homes. As the Mississippi River Commission (MRC) weighed the consequences of activating the floodway in April of 2011, the State of Missouri pursued a court injunction to stop the MRC from activating the floodway, which was finally denied by the U.S. Supreme Court on May 1, 2011 (Camillo, 2012, p. 89).

Given the significant controversy, the impact on future water resources management decisions on the Mississippi River, and the scientific opportunity to understand the hydro-dynamics of a large levee breach, the USGS initiated an effort to collect hydrodynamic and other associated data before, during, and after activation of the floodway.

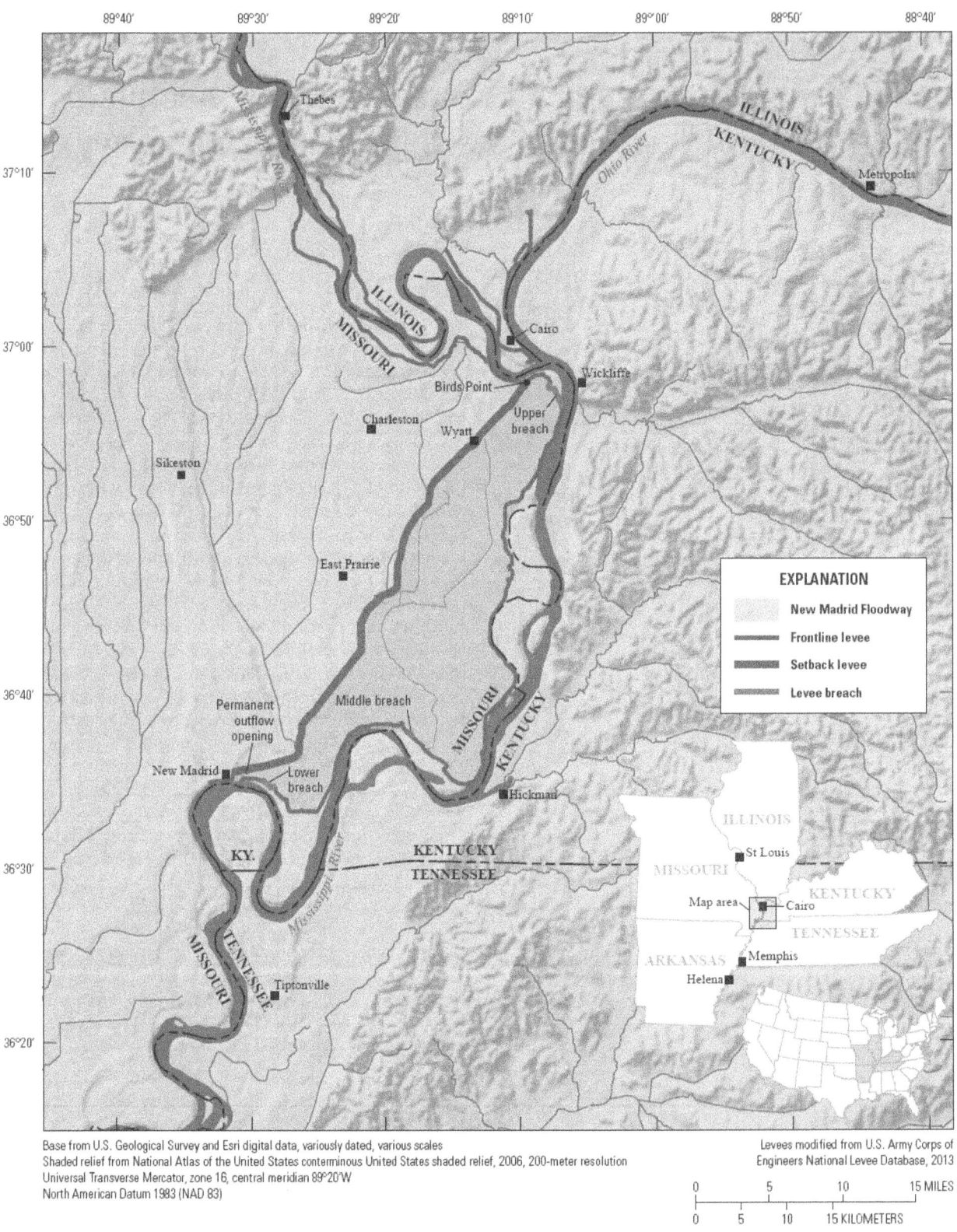

Figure 1.   The New Madrid Floodway study area.

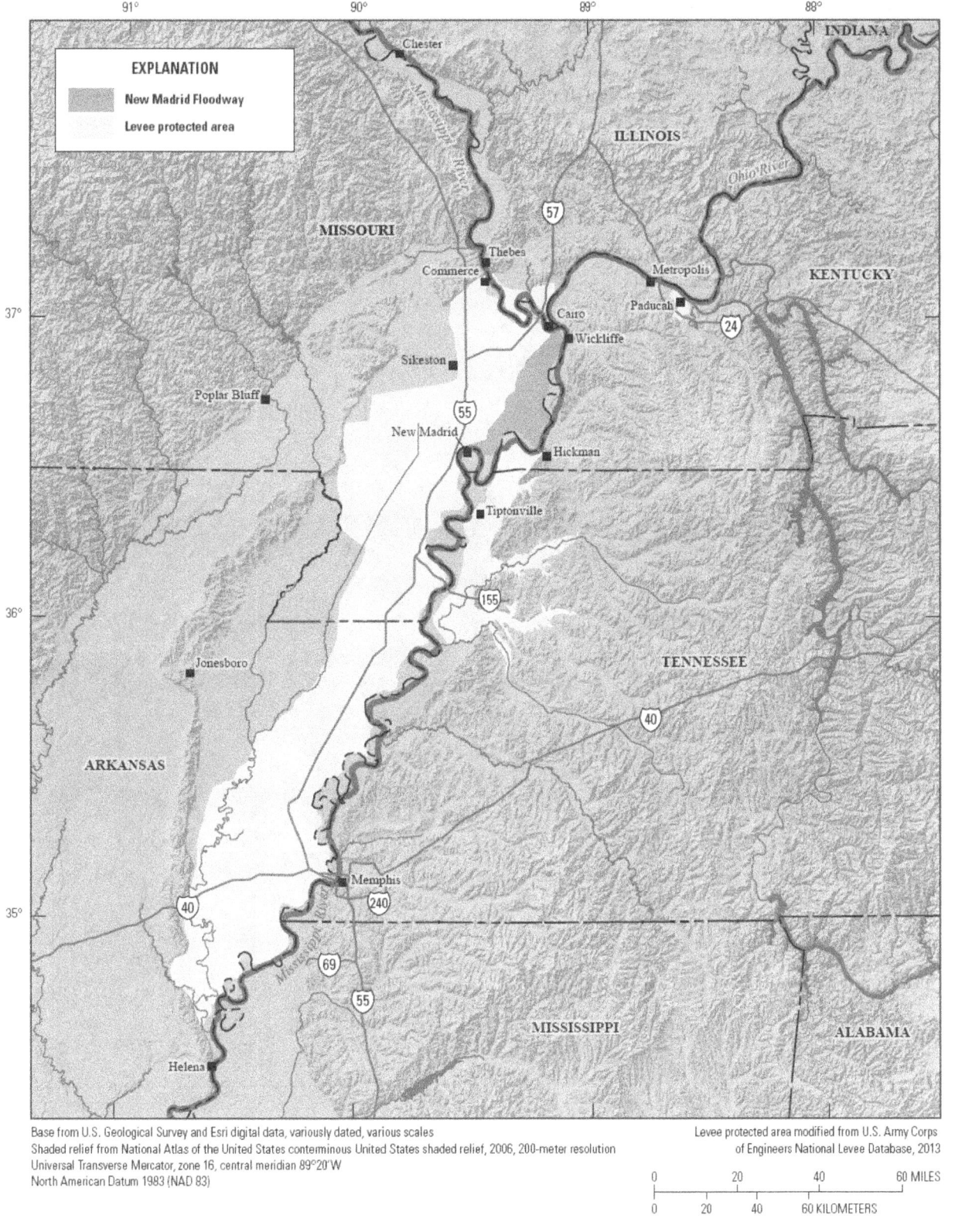

Figure 2.   Low-lying areas adjacent to the Mississippi and Ohio Rivers protected by the New Madrid Floodway.

USGS teams began making daily discrete observations of streamflow of the Mississippi and Ohio Rivers on April 28, 2011, at strategic locations upstream, downstream, and adjacent to the floodway. These measurements and ancillary data supported both the USACE flood fight efforts and the National Weather Service (NWS) river forecasting efforts. NWS forecasts of the flood magnitude and timing were crucial as the upstream flood waves coursing down the Mississippi and Ohio Rivers simultaneously arrived at the confluence area near Cairo, Ill. Given the unique opportunity to collect detailed data of the floodplain's hydraulic response to a levee breach, the USGS obtained access to the floodway from the State of Missouri and instrumented the floodway with autonomous submersible pressure transducers (SPTs), similar to the SPT shown in figure 3, in the event of floodway activation. On the evening of April 28, 2011, a USGS team deployed the first of 38 spatially distributed SPTs (fig. 4), each with the ability to collect a time series of water level data. The team finished deploying the last of these SPTs less than 24 hours later.

The USACE activated the floodway by detonating explosives just after 10:00 p m. on May 2, 2011, within a 9,000-foot section of levee at the upstream end near Birds Point (Camillo, 2012, p. 118, fig. 5). The activation of the floodway lowered the river stage at Cairo, Ill. by more than 0.4 feet in the first hour and nearly 1 foot in the first 6 hours (fig. 6). Comparisons of satellite images taken 7 months before the flood and 1 week after the activation of the floodway (fig. 7) demonstrate the immense capacity of the floodway as well as the extensive overbank flooding that existed during the period.

The purpose of this report is to present the data collected by the USGS in cooperation with the USACE in and near the floodway from April 28, 2011 to June 14, 2011. Methods used to collect and process these data also are presented.

Figure 3.   U.S. Geological Survey hydrologist installing a submersible pressure transducer in the New Madrid Floodway.

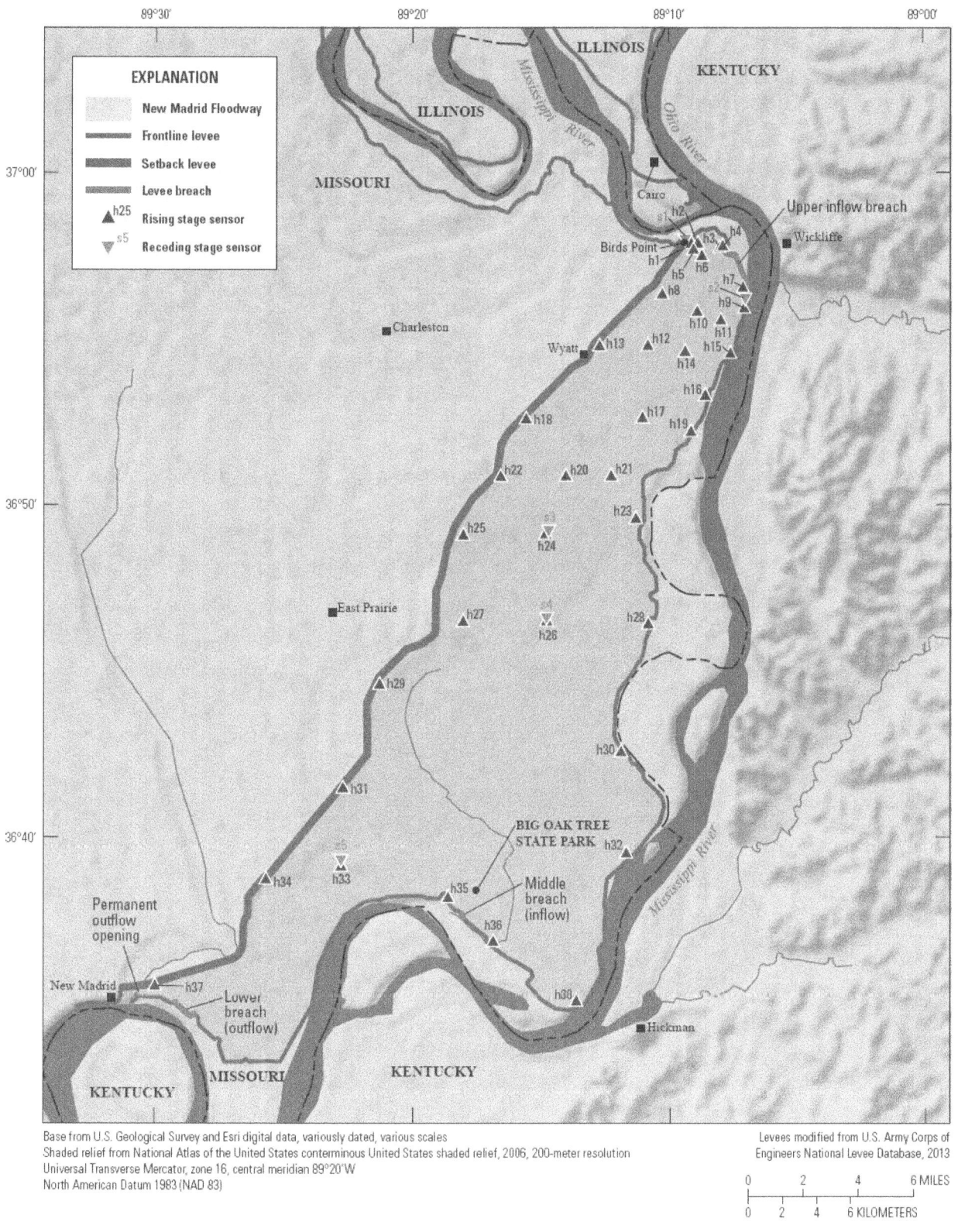

Figure 4. Map of the New Madrid Floodway showing 43 water level recording locations.

Figure 5. Detonation of the upper inflow fuse-plug levee near Birds Point at 10:03 p.m. on May 2, 2011.

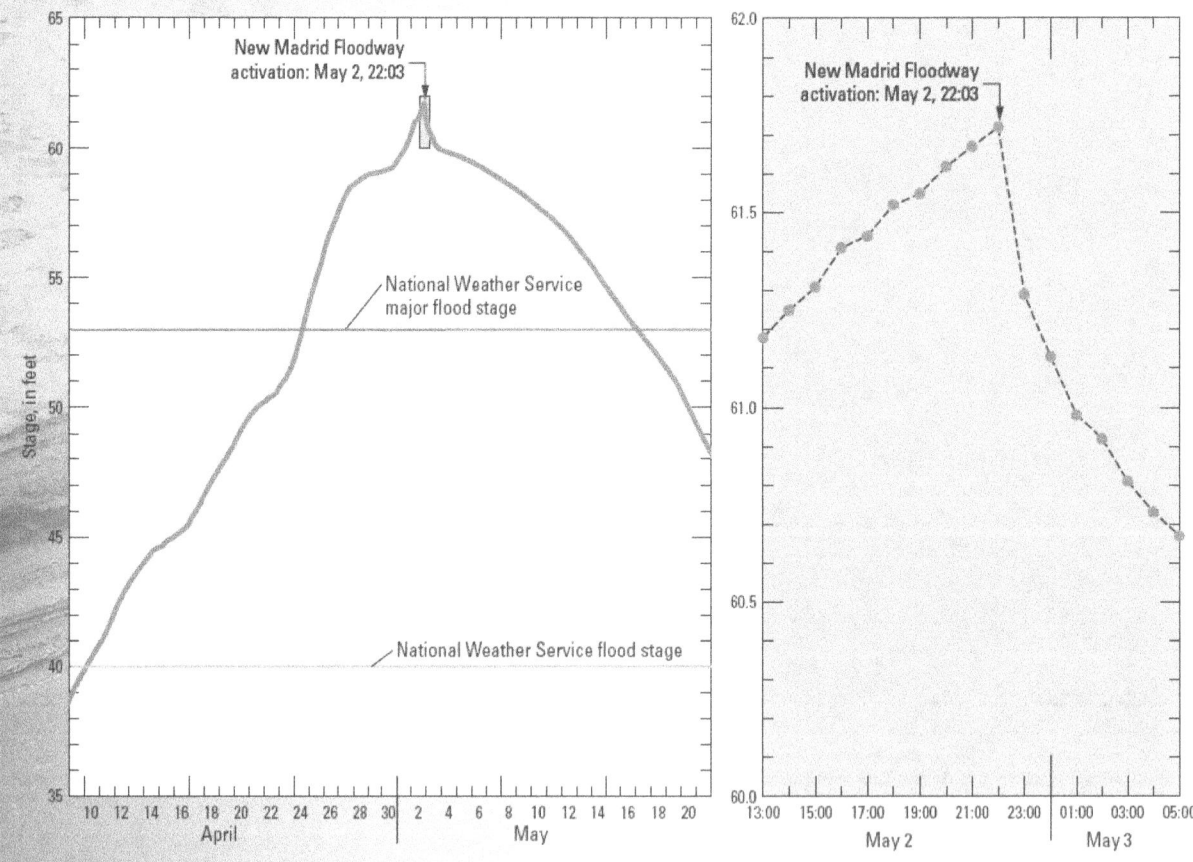

Figure 6. Stage hydrograph for the Ohio River at Cairo, Illinois (station number 365939089084601). Data from Jeanne Burns, U.S. Army Corps of Engineers, Hydraulics Branch, written commun., 2012.

A. October 14, 2010

B. May 10, 2011

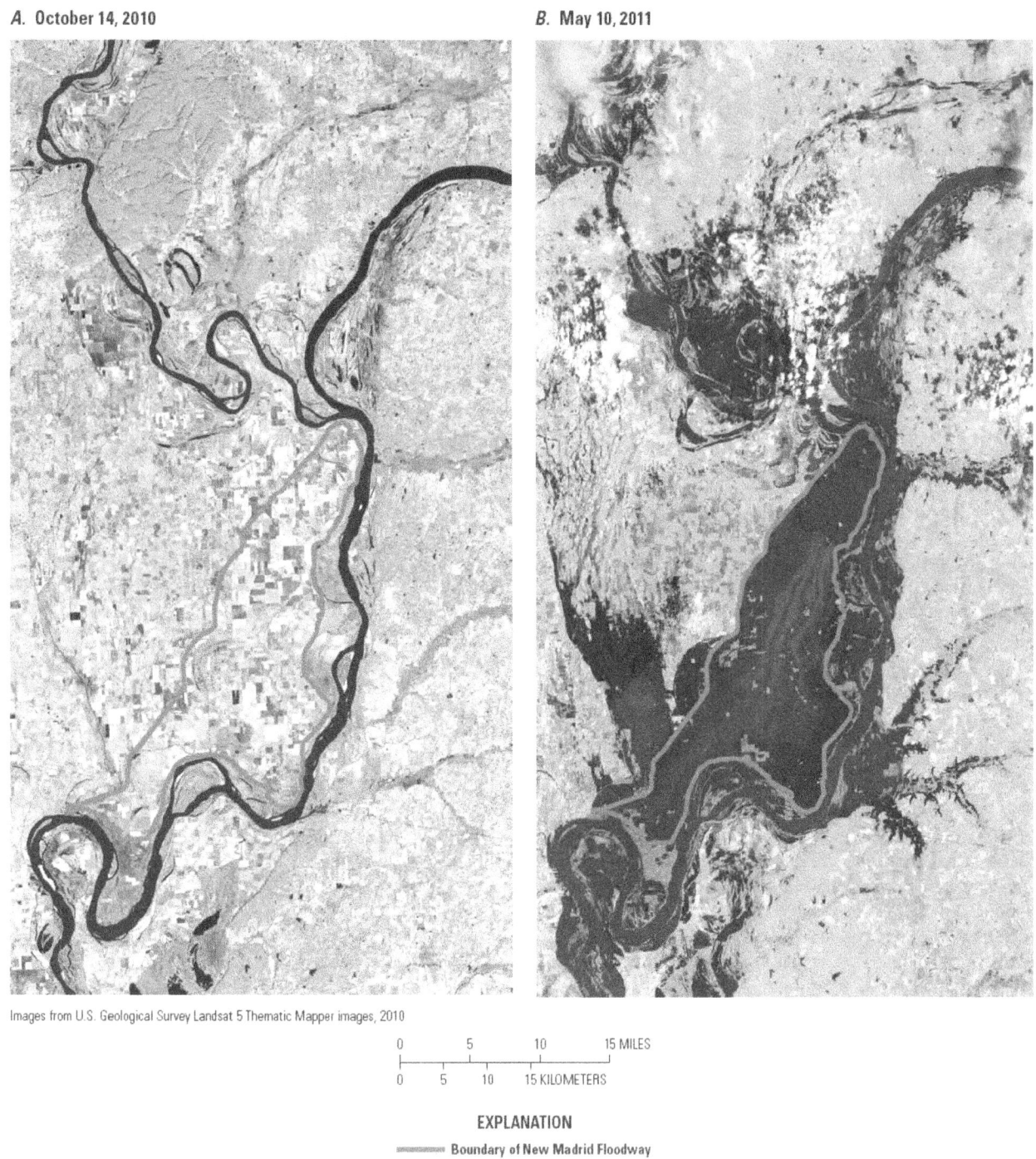

Images from U.S. Geological Survey Landsat 5 Thematic Mapper images, 2010

```
0        5        10       15 MILES
|----+----|----+----|----+----|
0        5        10    15 KILOMETERS
```

EXPLANATION

════ Boundary of New Madrid Floodway

Figure 7. Landsat satellite images showing the Ohio and Mississippi River confluence and New Madrid Floodway A, on October 14, 2010, before the 2011 floods and B, on May 10, 2011, after the activation of the floodway.

Methods for Assessing Hydrodynamics in the Area of the New Madrid Floodway

During the 2011 flooding, USGS data collection efforts in the floodway were focused primarily on the time series of water levels (stage) at selected points within the floodway, and velocity and streamflow in and around the floodway. Remote sensing data, including Landsat imagery, also were collected during and after the flood. After the water levels receded in the floodway, the USGS surveyed the elevation and position of, and retrieved the data from, each SPT and converted the stage measurements to water-surface elevation. USGS crews also collected hydrodynamic data (water velocity and streamflow) using real-time, boat-mounted acoustic Doppler current profilers (ADCPs; Mueller and Wagner, 2009) throughout the event period.

Stage Recording Within the Floodway

The opportunity to study the progression of a large-scale levee-breach induced flood wave through an area as large as the floodway is rare. USGS staff deployed SPTs throughout the floodway for the purpose of recording stage data (fig. 4). These data would provide details about the flooding process if activation was elected by the USACE. Data gathered from the SPTs would be useful for understanding dam and levee breaks, and for calibrating computer models designed to simulate them.

On April 28 and 29, 2011, USGS personnel placed 38 SPTs for sensing rising stage in the floodway (fig. 4). Six SPTs were placed in areas already inundated by backwater from the floodway's natural opening near New Madrid, Mo. and another five were placed in locations that became submerged prior to floodway activation on May 2. The remaining 27 SPTs were placed in locations that were not submerged until the activation. Three primary factors affected the choice of locations for the SPTs:

- Covering the entire length of the floodway with the 38 SPTs available

- Capturing more spatial density near the upper breach

- Mounting SPTs to structures that would not move during the event

The devices were programmed to record absolute pressure every 30 seconds and cease recording when their memory capacity was filled (approximately 14 days). In addition to the 38 rising-stage SPTs, 3 more SPTs were placed outside the reach of flood water for sensing barometric pressure, which is needed to compute the water elevations from the absolute pressures recorded by the submerged SPTs. McGee and others (2005) provides a description of how these data are used to compute water-surface elevations.

A typical SPT used in this study contains a ceramic pressure sensor, battery, storage memory, and optical interface, all within a factory-sealed, stainless steel container. An SPT is suspended inside a protective steel pipe with openings at the top and bottom to allow water to move freely around the SPT. A closeup photo of a typical SPT is shown in figure 8. Each SPT measures the absolute pressure surrounding the sensor at the nose of the SPT. The absolute pressure includes both water pressure and the barometric pressure above the water. Subtracting the barometric pressure from each absolute pressure reading results in a water pressure value that can be mathematically converted to water depth above the sensor (McGee and others, 2005). If the elevation of the sensor is known with some level of accuracy, then the water elevation throughout the time period can also be established with similar accuracy. The resulting dataset contains a time series of water elevation from the moment that each SPT became submerged until it stopped recording or the water receded below the sensor.

Figure 8. Submersible pressure transducer similar to that used in the New Madrid Floodway.

Because the original 38 SPTs would run out of memory prior to the flood recession, 5 additional SPTs were deployed in the floodway to record the receding water elevation beginning May 18. The smaller number of SPTs available for recording the water's recession resulted in a more geographically limited dataset than the rising water dataset (fig. 4). To ensure that these SPTs would record data for the duration of the recession, they were programmed to record data every 15 minutes from May 18 through their recovery by USGS personnel. Therefore, a total of 43 SPTs were installed in the floodway for the purpose of recording stage: 38 measuring the rise and 5 measuring the recession.

As the water levels in the floodway receded, recovery of the SPTs began in late May 2011 and concluded in mid-July 2011. During recovery, USGS personnel established durable reference marks that were surveyed to establish the elevation of each SPT (fig. 9). Photos and notes also were recorded and archived for each location.

As each SPT was returned to the USGS office, data were downloaded using an optical interface and analyzed against air pressure samples to produce water-depth time-series datasets. Survey crews used a Level II global navigation satellite system (GNSS) survey (Rydlund, 2012) to establish the elevation of each sensor above the North American Vertical Datum of 1988. Adding these elevations to the depth datasets resulted in water-surface elevation time-series datasets.

Because many datasets included an initial period of hours or days for which the sensor had not yet become submerged, each dataset was trimmed to retain only that part of the data representing measurable water elevation above the sensor. The trimmed water elevation datasets were exported into individual location datasets in comma-separated values (CSV) format and uploaded to the USGS National Water Information System (NWIS) (U.S. Geological Survey, 2008). Because the NWIS system loader can only accept 1 measurement for each 1-minute time slot, the 30-second data collected by the 38 SPTs as the floodway filled were generalized to 1-minute data as every other measurement was accepted by the loader. Analysis of the datasets indicates that this generalization resulted in no substantial loss of meaningful data.

One device in the dataset recorded no pressure readings greater than the surrounding barometric pressure, indicating that water never exceeded the elevation of 312.77 feet at that location (fig. 4, map site number h28). Consequently, there is no water elevation dataset available for this station, and only 37 water elevation datasets are available for the rising period.

The 15-minute data collected by the five receding period SPTs were processed in a similar manner as the rising period SPT data and stored in NWIS without time generalization. Thus, a total of 42 water level datasets are available: 37 for the rise and 5 for the recession.

Figure 9. A lag bolt used to mark the location and elevation of a recovered submersible pressure transducer.

Continuous Stage and Streamflow of the Mississippi and Ohio Rivers near the New Madrid Floodway

The important role of permanent streamgages should not be overlooked in any discussion on flooding. In the midst of the 2011 floods, long-term established streamgages provided real-time information to forecasters and decisionmakers regarding the status of river elevations and streamflow, both in their vicinity and at upstream locations. The NWS used the streamgage data to forecast critically important streamflows and stages. The reliability of NWS forecasts would be diminished without observed data from streamgages to validate and calibrate the forecast models (Mason and Weiger, 1995).

Discrete Hydrodynamic Measurements Within and Near the New Madrid Floodway

As the Mississippi and Ohio Rivers approached record flood levels in 2011, hydrodynamic measurements, including water velocity, depth, and streamflow rate, became indispensable for flood management and navigational safety while forming an important dataset for scientific study. The USGS deployed field crews to make frequent (sometimes daily) measurements of velocity, depth, and streamflow at key locations in and around the floodway. These locations included the inflow and outflow points of the floodway and several locations on the main stems of the Mississippi and Ohio Rivers, including flow across the adjacent floodplains (fig. 10).

The hydrodynamic measurements were made with boat-mounted ADCPs capable of measuring three-dimensional water velocities throughout the water column, along with the water depth and cross section width. When the value of the streamflow was desired, the velocity, depth, and width data were used to compute total streamflow rates.

Data from a typical ADCP measurement are shown in figure 11. As the downward-looking ADCP travels across the water surface, sound waves transmitted by the device are reflected by scatterers (typically suspended sediment) from the water column back to the device. The frequency shift detected by the ADCP in the return signal indicates the speed of the particles and thus the speed of the water at locations throughout the water column (Mueller and Wagner, 2009). The device also can determine water depth by listening for stronger return signals off the streambed. Cross section width also is determined by measuring boat speed and direction. By collecting and compiling these data, the ADCP software provides detailed riverbed profiles and three-dimensional velocity profiles at many locations in the cross section as the boat moves across the river. When streamflow measurement is desired, velocity measurements in each small subsection of the flow are multiplied by the area of each section and then summed for the entire cross section to compute a total streamflow in the river. A complete discussion of ADCP theory, as well as how these data are collected and presented, is provided by Mueller and Wagner (2009).

Routine streamflow measurements in normal river channels can be made quickly and consistently using ADCPs, but the extreme conditions presented during the 2011 flood added time and complexity to each measurement. Accurate measurement of the total streamflow of the Mississippi and Ohio Rivers required measurement of flow moving through large overbank areas in addition to the main channels. This required careful navigation through shallow waters and groves of vegetation, and frequent assessment of the data quality. When data quality was degraded, notes were taken and used during final processing of these data. Inside the floodway, swift flows near the inflow at Birds Point and the growth of a scour hole in the hours and days immediately following activation required special attention to detail and safety.

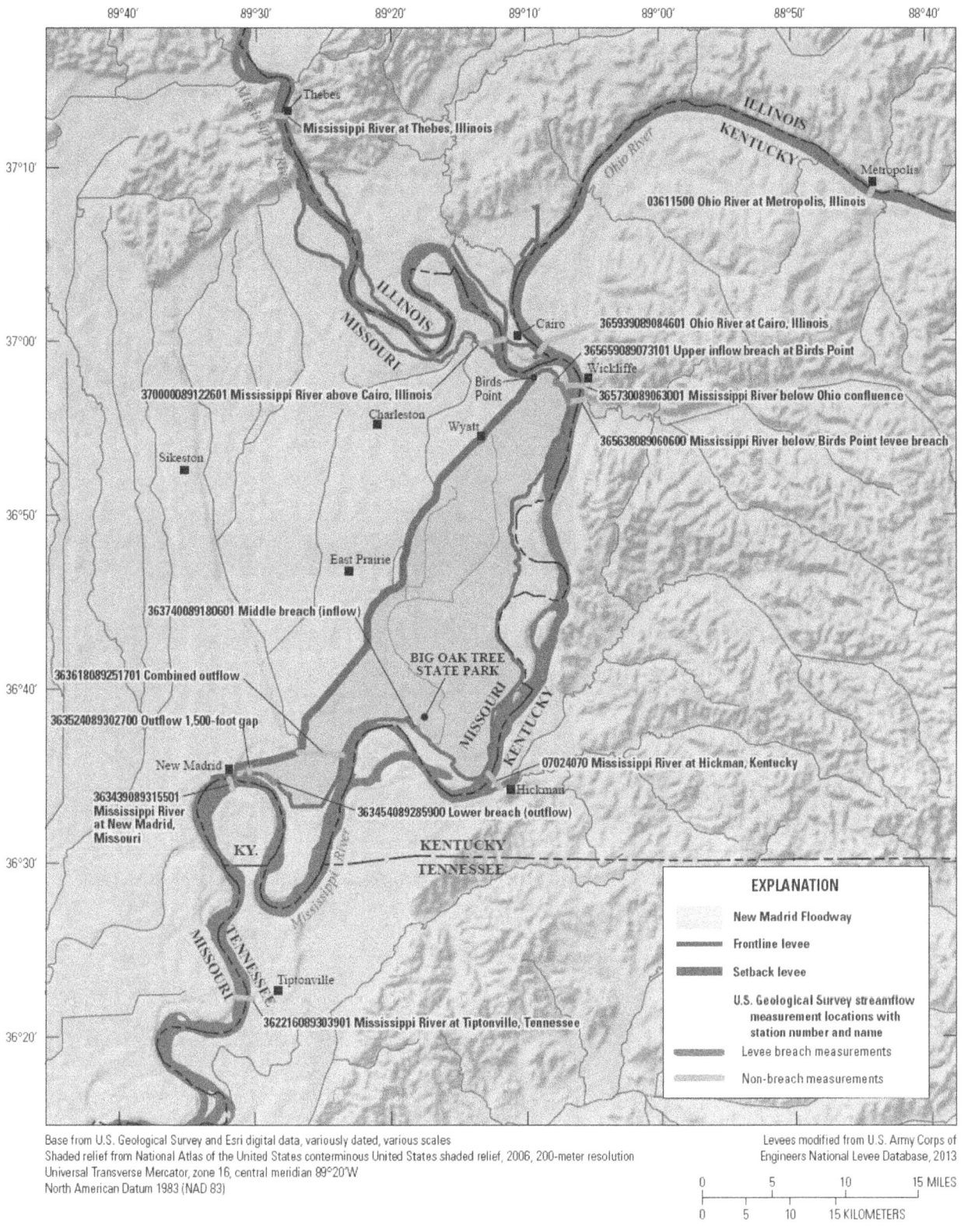

Figure 10. Approximate locations of streamflow measurements from April 28 to June 14, 2011, in and near the New Madrid Floodway.

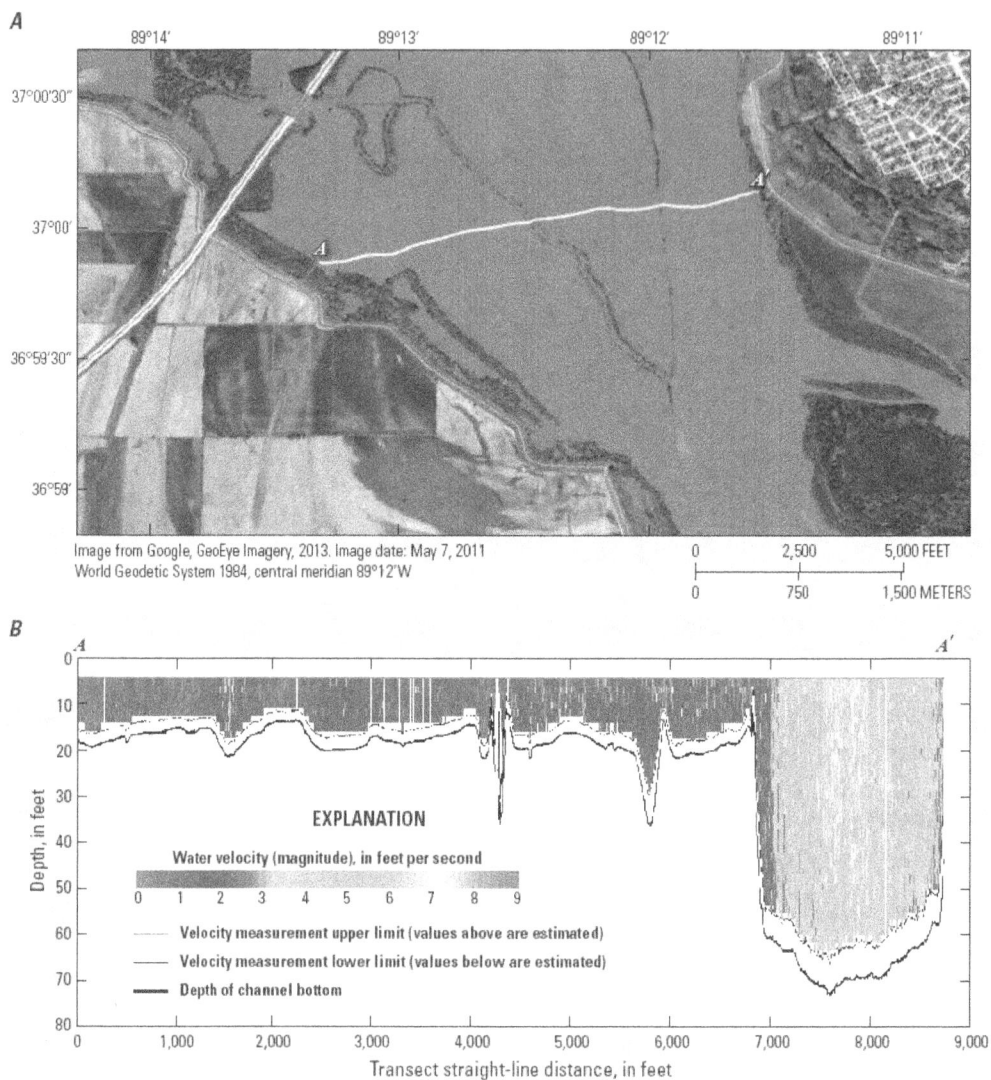

A

Image from Google, GeoEye Imagery, 2013. Image date: May 7, 2011
World Geodetic System 1984, central meridian 89°12'W

B

EXPLANATION

Water velocity (magnitude), in feet per second

0   1   2   3   4   5   6   7   8   9

——— Velocity measurement upper limit (values above are estimated)
——— Velocity measurement lower limit (values below are estimated)
—— Depth of channel bottom

Figure 11.   Example acoustic measurement transect at the Mississippi River above Cairo, Illinois (station number 370000089122601) including A, May 1, 2011 transect path drawn over May 7, 2011 satellite imagery (inundation similar to May 1), and B, cross-section graph of water velocity magnitudes collected during the transect.

The area near the confluence of the Ohio and Mississippi Rivers is hydrodynamically complicated. Two large rivers with a total drainage area of almost 903,000 square miles converge, both having large overbank areas (some as wide as 2 miles beyond the banks of the main channel). Within 1.5 miles below the confluence—less than the flooded width at that point—their total flow will split if the floodway is activated, potentially diverting as much as 22 percent of their combined flow through the floodway (Mississippi River Commission, 2012) . Because of the complex flow patterns through this area, particularly with the activation of the floodway, the USGS was asked to map the near-surface water velocities prior to and after the activation of the floodway. These velocity maps, available at *http://water.usgs.gov/floods/events/2011/BPNM/data_archive/*, assisted the U.S. Coast Guard in determining if navigation traffic could safely pass near the floodway after the activation. Changes in the magnitude and direction of flows of the Mississippi and Ohio Rivers could have resulted in a dangerous situation for shipping traffic, particularly in the reach around the bridges at Cairo and in the immediate vicinity of Birds Point where the water was being diverted. The USGS observations indicated no appreciable changes in water velocity magnitude and direction near the shipping channels, enabling the U.S. Coast Guard to confidently open that stretch of the Mississippi River to navigation traffic after the last floodway detonation.

Streamflow measurements were made upstream from the confluence near Cairo for the Mississippi River (station number 370000089122601) and for the Ohio River (station number 365939089084601) (fig. 10). Each measurement consisted of a main channel part and an overflow part as a result of the high flood stages of the rivers. Main channel measurements in these areas were fairly routine, despite the dangers of swift flows and river traffic. Overbank areas for both locations were large and difficult to measure. As explained in the Measurement Locations section of this report, the eastern overbanks of the Ohio River proved difficult to measure during the first few days of measurements. Likewise, overflows of the Mississippi River proved challenging as waters receded.

Prior to the activation of the floodway, crews made measurements of the combined upper Mississippi River and Ohio River flows at a location just downstream from the confluence near Wickliffe, Kentucky (station number 365730089063001) (fig. 10); however, this location was coincident with the location of the levee fuse plug at Birds Point and thus coincident with the inflow to the floodway once it was activated. Accurately differentiating the streamflow split between the Mississippi River and floodway anywhere along the activated fuse plug at this location would be impossible after the activation. As a result, after the floodway was activated on May 2, measurement crews moved to station number 365638089060600, immediately downstream from the breach. When combined with the streamflow measurements inside the upper inflow breach (365659089073101), these three stations represent the total flow immediately below the confluence of the Mississippi and Ohio Rivers. To summarize all three components, station

number 07022300 was created for a location near Wickliffe. More information about the relation among these four station numbers can be found in the Measurement Locations section and table 3 of this report.

Hydrodynamic Data Associated With the Activation of the New Madrid Floodway

The data presented in this report have been posted to the USGS Flood Information Web site at *http://water.usgs.gov/floods/events/2011/BPNM/data_archive/*, which is called the "data archive" in the remainder of this document. In addition, much of the stage and streamflow data described here have also been posted for permanent archival and public access in the USGS NWISweb service, accessible at *http://waterdata.usgs.gov/*. The remainder of this report describes in detail the information that is available in these two locations.

Stages Within the New Madrid Floodway After Activation

Time-series water-surface elevation data for 42 floodway SPTs are available in the data archive. The posted CSV file for each SPT contains station number, date/time, and water-surface elevation at 1-minute intervals (during rise) or 15-minute intervals (during recession), as shown in the example in figure 12.

365538089080001,05/02/2011 22:23,310.58
365538089080001,05/02/2011 22:24,310.65
365538089080001,05/02/2011 22:25,310.79
365538089080001,05/02/2011 22:26,310.94
365538089080001,05/02/2011 22:27,311.10

Figure 12. Example contents from New Madrid Floodway comma-separated values (CSV) file showing station number, date/time, and water-surface elevation.

Every record includes the station number, which allows the user to avoid ambiguity among SPTs when combining multiple CSV files for time-series analysis. An additional CSV file has been provided, which includes the station number, latitude, longitude, sensor elevation, and elevation uncertainty of each SPT. In addition, links to online and downloadable maps of the data collection locations are provided on the USGS Flood Information Web site. The USGS NWISweb service also allows the user to download similar data. Using NWISweb, users can quickly generate hydrographs and see mapped locations for each SPT.

Users of the time-series stage data described above will notice a number of interesting characteristics in the data, some of which are described here. One of the most noticeable characteristics is the variation in the time when water first began to rise past each SPT sensor. As would be expected, SPTs nearer the detonated upper inflow fuse-plug levee documented rising water-level elevations sooner than those farther downstream. Additional factors affecting when each sensor became inundated include the variation in topography and the associated mounting elevations of each SPT.

The variation in the initial rates of rise of the water elevation also is notable. The difference in response between two SPTs in different locations of the floodway is illustrated in figure 13. Some SPTs, such as station number 363514089134101 in figure 13 (fig. 4, map site number h38) were placed in an area of backwater (typically at the southern end of the floodway) and submerged long before the upper inflow breach was initiated. The data from these SPTs indicate a more gradual increase in water elevation from rising backwaters until the breach inflows accelerate the rise in stage. SPTs that display a sharp beginning rise in water-surface elevation, such as station

number 365757089090901 (fig. 4, map site number h1), were dry until floodway activation caused faster water level rises.

The rate of rise at various locations also may be of interest when studying the behavior of the floodway. Maximum rates of rise were computed for all 37 SPTs measuring the rise and listed in table 1. The table shows each station with its fastest periods of 5-minute, 15-minute, and 1-hour rates of rise. For convenient comparison, each rate is listed in feet per minute. The greatest 5-minute rise of 2.55 feet occurred at station number 365242089110501 (fig. 4, map site number h17). The rise occurred more than 2 hours after the activation and nearly 6 miles away from the inflow breach. The greatest 15-minute rise of 5.21 feet was measured at station number 365751089080301 (fig. 4, map site number h3), just 20 minutes after activation, about 1,000 feet from the inflow breach. The greatest 1-hour rise of 8.12 feet occurred at station number 365538089080001 (fig. 4, map site number h11), about 80 minutes after the activation and more than 1 mile from the breach.

In addition to the patterns mentioned already, the data include noticeable concurrent small rises across many SPTs, which may indicate a rain event. As previously noted, users also may notice the empty dataset from station number 364629089105201 (fig. 4, map site number h28), indicating that this sensor was never submerged at all.

Table 2 summarizes the data available from the 43 SPTs. This table includes the following information:

- Map site number corresponding to locations in figure 4 map.

- 15-digit USGS station number for finding data on NWISweb.

- Latitude and longitude of the station location.

- Elevation of the SPT sensor.

- Date/time sensor first became submerged.

- Peak water-surface elevation, and the date and time of occurrence.

- Uncertainty associated with each dataset.

The water-surface elevations reported in the datasets are dependent on the accurate measurement of water depth and the accurate measurement of the each SPTs elevation. Therefore, the uncertainty mentioned in the list above is composed of two main sources: (1) the uncertainty related to the SPTs measurement accuracy and (2) the uncertainty associated with determining the SPTs elevation. The first measure is fairly straightforward since the manufacturer reports the accuracy of the devices as +/- 0.015 feet for the application used in this study. Thus, it is assumed that any elevation reported in the dataset is within 0.015 feet of the true value relative to other values recorded by that same SPT; however, when comparing a given value to other SPTs or other applications outside of this study, the uncertainty of the device's elevation also

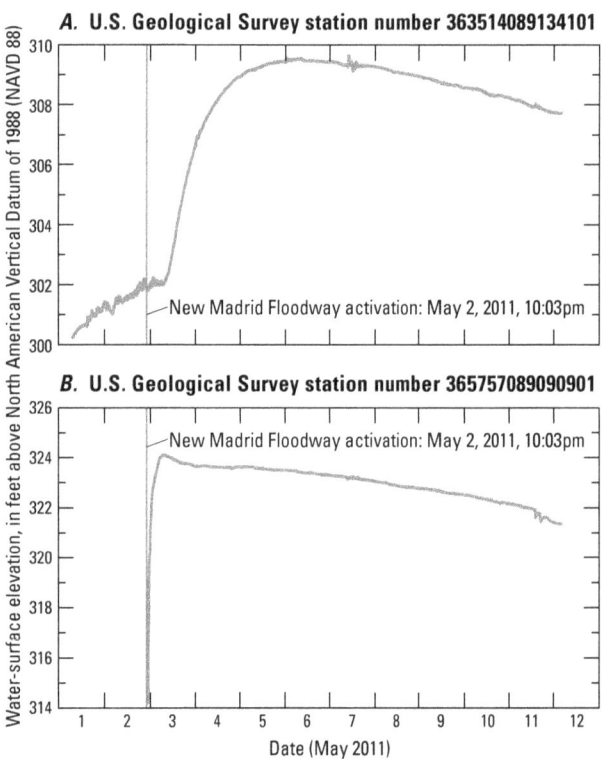

Figure 13.   Water-surface elevation hydrographs for *A*, station experiencing natural backwater effects prior to New Madrid Floodway activation and *B*, station experiencing first submersion resulting from New Madrid Floodway activation.

Table 1.   Maximum rates of water level rise, in feet per minute, for locations in the New Madrid Floodway.

[All values rounded to hundredths of a foot per minute. Bold red values indicate maxima in each category]

Station number	5-minute rise	ending at:	15-minute rise	ending at:	1-hour rise	ending at:
365757089090901	0.24	May-02 23:08	0.22	May-02 23:12	0.11	May-02 23:56
365757089085401	0.18	May-02 22:54	0.16	May-02 23:03	0.10	May-02 23:48
365751089080301	0.43	May-02 22:17	0.35	May-02 22:24	0.13	May-02 23:06
365751089080101	0.08	May-02 22:36	0.06	May-02 22:46	0.03	May-03 00:31
365745089090401	0.18	May-02 23:09	0.16	May-02 23:11	0.10	May-02 23:46
365734089084501	0.30	May-02 22:36	0.17	May-02 22:46	0.09	May-02 23:31
365637089070601	0.24	May-02 22:33	0.16	May-02 22:33	0.08	May-02 23:18
365625089101701	0.29	May-02 23:33	0.18	May-02 23:43	0.08	May-03 00:28
365559089065501	0.06	May-03 00:08	0.04	May-03 00:02	0.03	May-03 00:28
365553089085601	0.28	May-02 22:36	0.18	May-02 23:17	0.13	May-02 23:29
365538089080001	0.48	May-02 22:35	0.32	May-02 22:41	0.14	May-02 23:23
365452089105201	0.10	May-03 00:30	0.05	May-03 00:40	0.02	May-03 01:25
365451089124501	0.09	May-03 02:28	0.07	May-03 01:47	0.04	May-03 02:33
365441089092401	0.30	May-02 23:51	0.14	May-03 00:01	0.08	May-03 00:46
365438089072901	0.28	May-02 22:51	0.23	May-02 22:56	0.12	May-02 23:30
365321089082901	0.25	May-02 23:32	0.21	May-02 23:34	0.13	May-03 00:00
365242089110501	0.51	May-03 00:50	0.25	May-03 01:00	0.12	May-03 01:45
365239089153701	0.06	May-03 04:33	0.04	May-03 04:40	0.02	May-03 05:25
365216089091101	0.21	May-03 00:17	0.11	May-03 00:27	0.07	May-03 01:12
365057089140401	0.31	May-03 03:28	0.22	May-03 03:38	0.09	May-03 04:23
365057089121801	0.09	May-03 03:19	0.06	May-03 04:00	0.05	May-03 03:19
365056089163601	0.02	May-11 14:13	0.01	May-11 14:13	0.00	May-07 10:58
364939089112101	0.05	May-03 04:44	0.04	May-03 04:55	0.02	May-03 05:42
364912089145201	0.12	May-03 04:34	0.11	May 03 04:39	0.07	May-03 05:22
364910089180401	0.21	May-03 07:10	0.13	May-03 07:19	0.07	May-03 08:04
364635089145003	0.04	May-03 02:03	0.04	May-03 02:15	0.03	May-03 02:42
364634089180501	0.05	May-03 06:45	0.04	May-03 06:45	0.03	May-03 07:21
364441089211901	0.02	Apr-30 22:50	0.01	May-03 09:56	0.01	May-03 09:21
364238089115601	0.04	May-07 12:46	0.02	May-07 12:46	0.00	May-07 12:51
364133089224401	0.06	May-07 12:49	0.02	May-07 13:19	0.01	May-03 14:40
363935089114401	0.05	May-06 01:14	0.02	May-06 01:24	0.01	May-03 14:16
363912089224801	0.12	May-02 17:58	0.04	May-02 00:29	0.01	Apr-30 13:41
363849089254201	0.05	May-07 13:19	0.02	May-07 13:29	0.01	May-03 16:33
363816089184001	0.03	May-01 23:49	0.02	May-01 15:34	0.01	May-03 13:24
363653089170701	0.06	May-04 00:38	0.02	May-04 01:23	0.01	May-04 00:55
363537089300001	0.04	May-03 12:41	0.01	May-03 12:41	0.01	May-03 12:41
363514089134101	0.05	May-02 20:34	0.02	May-01 14:58	0.01	May-03 14:54

Table 2. Summary of temporary stage recorder data.

[USGS, U.S. Geological Survey; n/a, not applicable]

Map site number (fig. 4)	USGS station number	Station latitude (decimal degrees)	Station longitude (decimal degrees)	Sensor elevation (feet)	Date and time sensor first submerged	Peak water elevation (feet)	Date and time of peak water elevation	Water elevation uncertainty (feet)
h1	365757089090901	36.96572	-89.15260	314.24	May 02 22:56	324.10	May 03 07:40	0.13
h2	365757089085401	36.96573	-89.14837	314.31	May 02 22:48	324.24	May 03 06:39	0.13
h3	365751089080301	36.96411	-89.13415	311.83	May 02 14:13	324.17	May 03 07:03	0.13
h4	365751089080101	36.96404	-89.13371	318.07	May 02 22:29	324.24	May 03 06:51	0.14
h5	365745089090401	36.96262	-89.15118	314.30	May 02 22:46	324.24	May 03 06:55	0.13
h6	365734089084501	36.95947	-89.14582	314.01	May 02 22:31	324.16	May 03 06:52	0.13
h7	365637089070601	36.94361	-89.11839	314.35	May 02 22:11	325.01	May 03 07:47	0.20
h8	365625089101701	36.94017	-89.17137	316.40	May 02 23:28	323.69	May 03 07:10	0.05
h9	365559089065501	36.93317	-89.11519	319.09	May 02 23:16	323.76	May 03 07:10	0.25
h10	365553089085601	36.93140	-89.14893	308.90	Apr 29 06:00	323.86	May 03 06:54	0.05
h11	365538089080001	36.92712	-89.13342	308.86	Apr 29 01:00	323.78	May 03 07:00	0.05
h12	365452089105201	36.91454	-89.18101	318.25	May 03 00:25	322.52	May 03 07:41	0.05
h13	365451089124501	36.91428	-89.21237	316.51	May 03 01:32	321.89	May 03 08:22	0.12
h14	365441089092401	36.91140	-89.15670	315.81	May 02 23:46	323.09	May 03 07:27	0.05
h15	365438089072901	36.91050	-89.12473	309.88	May 02 04:09	323.14	May 03 07:24	0.13
h16	365321089082901	36.88925	-89.14148	310.49	May 02 22:53	322.70	May 03 07:29	0.19
h17	365242089110501	36.87820	-89.18468	310.23	May 03 00:45	321.63	May 03 07:29	0.12
h18	365239089153701	36.87762	-89.26019	312.72	May 03 04:25	314.64	May 03 08:46	0.12
h19	365216089091101	36.87124	-89.15311	311.78	May 03 00:12	321.79	May 03 07:31	0.27
h20	365057089140401	36.84906	-89.23453	304.91	May 03 03:23	313.20	May 05 15:45	0.09
h21	365057089121801	36.84906	-89.20502	302.52	May 01 15:23	313.45	May 05 15:05	0.12
h22	365056089163601	36.84885	-89.27669	310.91	May 04 02:15	311.93	May 05 16:15	0.09
h23	364939089112101	36.82763	-89.18919	309.67	May 03 04:34	312.63	May 05 15:24	0.51
h24	364912089145201	36.82003	-89.24777	301.93	May 03 04:13	311.60	May 05 23:05	0.09
h25	364910089180401	36.81946	-89.30117	302.66	May 03 07:04	311.36	May 06 15:43	0.09
h26	364635089145003	36.77627	-89.24729	302.18	May 02 23:03	311.06	May 06 10:16	0.03
h27	364634089180501	36.77607	-89.30139	300.75	May 01 02:01	310.84	May 06 15:06	0.03
h28	364629089105201	36.77480	-89.18110	312.77	n/a	n/a	n/a	n/a
h29	364441089211901	36.74464	-89.35527	299.02	Apr 29 14:08	310.24	May 06 15:43	0.07
h30	364238089115601	36.71067	-89.19896	308.77	May 04 17:44	309.80	May 07 12:46	0.14
h31	364133089224401	36.69262	-89.37885	303.69	May 03 12:57	309.74	May 07 12:49	0.07
h32	363935089114401	36.65982	-89.19562	303.40	May 03 12:33	309.71	May 06 01:03	0.25
h33	363912089224801	36.65340	-89.37999	299.86	Apr 29 11:44	309.00	May 06 06:39	0.02
h34	363849089254201	36.64684	-89.42821	303.67	May 03 14:29	308.84	May 07 12:57	0.02
h35	363816089184001	36.63776	-89.31123	298.72	Apr 29 16:52	309.47	May 06 05:49	0.07
h36	363653089170701	36.61464	-89.28537	305.40	May 03 18:46	309.52	May 06 06:44	0.14
h37	363537089300001	36.59357	-89.49989	302.62	May 03 10:42	306.40	May 05 20:41	0.03
h38	363514089134101	36.58725	-89.22795	300.22	May 01 07:06	309.64	May 07 09:55	0.10
s1	365758089092301	36.96611	-89.15636	314.24	n/a	318.43	May 18 20:00	0.13
s2	365610089065601	36.93619	-89.11551	314.60	n/a	318.01	May 18 16:00	0.24
s3	364912089144501	36.82006	-89.24586	300.02	n/a	306.83	May 18 08:15	0.09
s4	364635089145001	36.77627	-89.24729	301.29	n/a	305.67	May 18 08:15	0.03
s5	363912089224803	36.65340	-89.37999	294.21	n/a	303.88	May 18 08:15	0.02

must be taken into account. As shown in table 2, the total uncertainty ranges from 0.02 feet to 0.27 feet, except for station number 364939089112101 (fig. 4, map site number h23, discussed below), with the average being about 0.12 feet. The sources of this uncertainty included the uncertainty in the Global Positioning System (GPS) survey of nearby reference marks, which ranged from less than 0.01 feet to 0.25 feet, and the uncertainty in the leveling methods and equipment used to relate the sensor elevations to those reference marks, which was in the range of 0 to 0.01 feet. In the special case of station number 364939089112101 (fig. 4, map site number h23), evidence during recovery indicated that the device had been disturbed just prior to recovery (after data collection had ceased), increasing the uncertainty in the vertical location of the device and thus the true elevations of the data. As a result, the original location was estimated from photos, adding about 0.3 feet to its uncertainty.

Continuous Stage and Streamflow Data

USGS and USACE real-time streamgage data as well as archives of 2011 flood data are available on the agencies' respective Web sites. USGS streamgage data can be found at *http://waterdata.usgs.gov*. In addition, the USGS has posted selected CSV file archives for the 2011 flood period on their flood webpage at *http://water.usgs.gov/floods/events/2011/ BPNM/data_archive/*. Most USACE streamgage data can be found at *http://www.rivergages.com*. Some data only are available by contacting the USACE Memphis District.

Discrete Observations of Streamflow, Velocity, and Depth

In addition to the time series of water-surface elevation data described previously, the USGS has provided a collection of discrete observations of streamflow, including hydrodynamic velocity and depth data, in the data archive at *http:// water.usgs.gov/floods/events/2011/BPNM/data_archive/*. Visitors to this Web site will find detailed data files for measurements made in the floodway at each of the inflow and outflow locations, as well as main stem Mississippi and Ohio River locations around the floodway area as shown in figure 10. A georeferenced file named "BPNM_streamflow.kml" containing the locations shown in figure 10 also is available on the Web site. The kml format is a popular XML-based format that can be imported easily into many mapping and Geographic Information System applications. The locations shown in the "BPNM_streamflow.kml" file indicate the approximate sections where ADCP measurements were made. A detailed summary of these measurements can be found in table 4 at the back of this report.

Measurement Locations

Floodway inflow measurements are presented for the inflow at the upper inflow breach near Birds Point (station number 365659089073101) as well as for the middle inflow breach near Big Oak Tree State Park (station number 363740089180601) as shown in figure 10. The upper inflow near Birds Point was the primary inflow for the floodway, with a peak diversion of more than 400,000 ft^3/s from the main stem of the Mississippi River in the early period of activation. The middle inflow breach was activated on the afternoon of May 5. This inflow contributed less than 90,000 ft^3/s at any given time, but contributed more than one-half of the inflow after May 17 as the inflow from the upper breach tapered off. ADCP streamflow measurements for both locations were made primarily on the inside of the floodway with hydrographers taking a variety of paths across the breaches to capture the bathymetry of the scour holes developing day-to-day. It should be noted that the streamflow measured at the upper inflow (station number 365659089083101) is a component of the total streamflow summarized at Wickliffe (station number 07022300) as described later in this section.

Outflow measurements are presented for the lower outflow breach (station number 363454089285900) and the natural 1,500-foot outflow opening of the floodway (station number 363524089302700) near New Madrid. On May 3, the total streamflow exiting the floodway was determined by measuring these two sections separately and then adding the results. On the next day, however, measuring crews discovered that safer and more accurate measurements could be made 3 miles to the northeast where State Highway P crosses a narrow section of the floodway. Single streamflow measurements at this location (station number 363618089251701) were considered equivalent to the combined measurements made downstream because all water flowing from either outflow had to first flow past this location before exiting the floodway. Measurements continued here until May 30, 2012, when water levels dropped below navigable depth and separate measurements had to be made once again at the two outflows. When depths here reached levels that were no longer measurable with a powered boat, crews moved one more time back to station number 363618089251701 to make the final 11 streamflow measurements from June 6 to June 14. At this location, flows were now reduced to a single channel with a bridge from which tethered ADCP streamflow measurements could be made.

The hydrographs in figure 14 depict the total inflows versus total outflows through the floodway from the end of April, just prior to activation, until mid-June when the diversion flow ceased. Data used to create these graphs are available on the USGS Flood Information Web site at *http://water.usgs. gov/floods/events/2011/BPNM/data_archive/* and the USGS NWISweb Web site at *http://waterdata.usgs.gov/*.

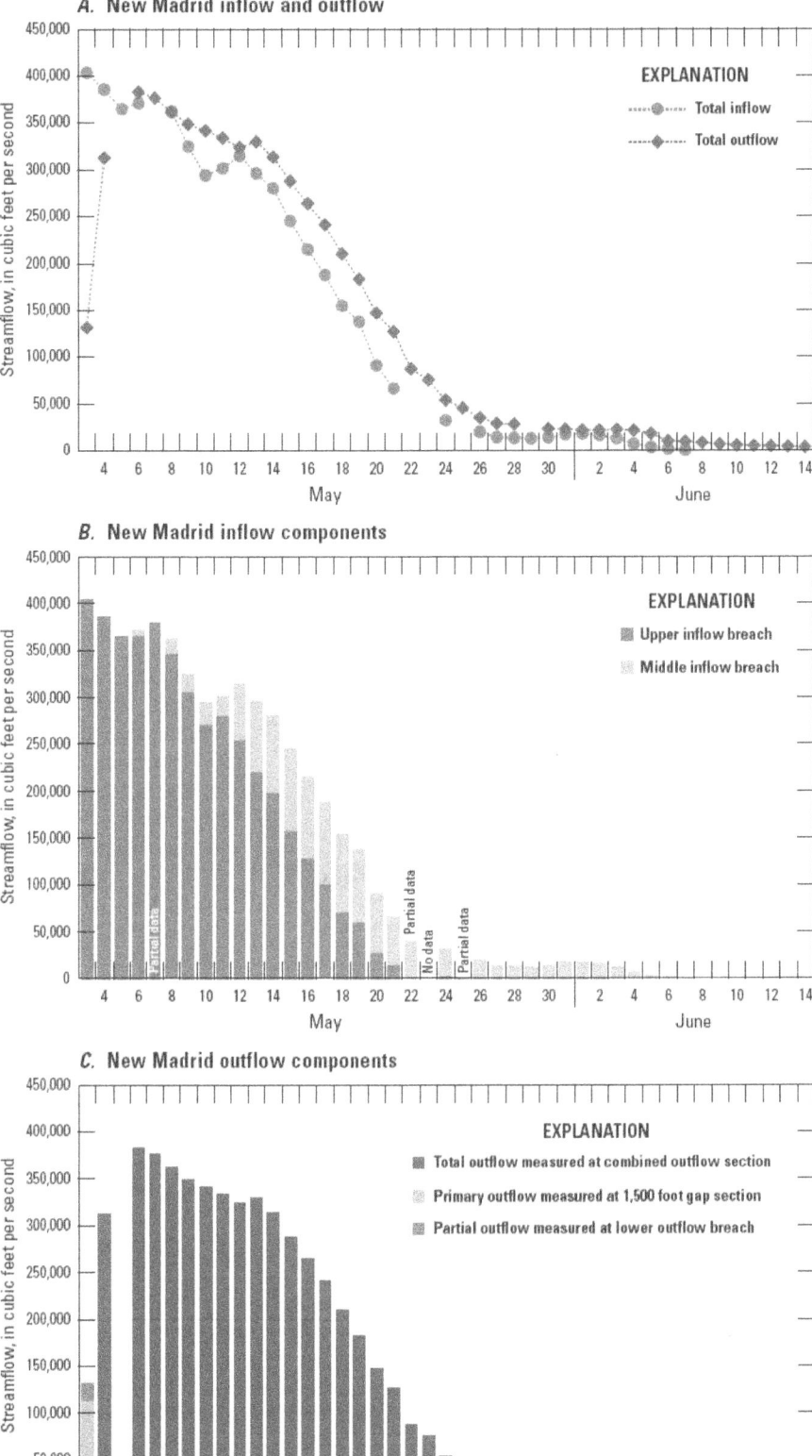

Figure 14. Hydrographs of the New Madrid Floodway showing *A*, a comparison of the total inflows and total outflows, *B*, the components of the total inflow, and *C*, the components of the total outflow.

The same types of data collected for the inflow and outflow locations also were collected for main stem locations along the Ohio and Mississippi Rivers near their confluence. These streamflow measurements are summarized in table 4. As previously noted, measurement locations on the Ohio River upstream from the confluence (station number 365939089084601) often contained difficult overflow sections that required several hours to measure, thus reducing the measurement quality. Main channel measurements were reliable, but boat crews struggled to find valid overbank measurement sections until May 4. To complete the earlier measurements, an overflow estimation method was developed after the floods by comparing the total streamflow data from the upstream gage at Metropolis, Ill. (station number 03611500) to the valid overflow measurements made after May 3. A strong linear relation (R^2 greater than 0.98) was found between these two parameters and applied to the entire period to estimate overflows on days where a valid main channel measurement was made without a valid overflow measurement. Each resulting overflow estimate represented less than 20 percent of the total streamflow and allowed reasonable estimates of total streamflow on those days. Estimated measurements are labeled accordingly in table 4. Measurement files and estimates also are available in the data archive.

Overflow estimates also were needed on the Mississippi River above Cairo (station number 370000089122601). The missing overflow measurements on the Mississippi River were estimated by interpolating results from other measurement days. Estimated measurements are labeled accordingly in table 4 at the end of this report. Details of those estimates can be found in the data archive.

As described earlier in this report, streamflow measurements of the uppermost point on the lower Mississippi River (just below the confluence of the Ohio and Mississippi Rivers) near Wickliffe were made in two different locations: station number 365730089063001 and station number 365638089060600. When combined with the streamflow measurements inside the Upper Inflow Breach (365659089073101), these three stations represent the total flow immediately below the confluence of the Mississippi and Ohio Rivers. Thus, there are three measurement locations for streamflow near Wickliffe. To simplify and summarize all three components, station number 07022300 was created for this location near Wickliffe. Users interested in the streamflow for the Mississippi River near Wickliff (which is the combination of the main channel, overbank flow outside the floodway, and that water diverted through the floodway) can use this NWIS station identification to find the total flow. Streamflow values found at station number 07022300 will either be a duplication of station number 365730089063001 or a combination of station numbers 365638089060600 and 36569089073101, depending on the date of measurement. Table 3 summarizes the relation among these four station numbers. Detailed files, described in the next section, can be found on the USGS Flood Information Web site for the three 15-digit stations, whereas summary data on NWISweb can be found for all four stations listed above.

Table 3. Diagram relating streamflow measurement stations on the Mississippi River near Wickliffe, Kentucky.

Prior to May 2 activation	After May 2 activation	
365730089063001 Mississippi River below Ohio confluence (Main stem and overflows)	365638089060600 Mississippi River below Birds Point levee (Main stem and overflows)	
	365659089073101 New Madrid Floodway upper inflow breach at Birds Point (Diverted floodway streamflow)	
07022300 Mississippi River near Wickliffe, Kentucky (Summary of all flows)		

Types of Data Files

The types of streamflow measurement data files are listed here and described in more detail below:

- Measurement summaries showing total streamflow, average velocity, and other details (.pdf)

- Raw, vendor-specific ADCP measurement data files: (.PD0, .mmt, .riv, and .wsp files)

- Measurement export files (_ASC.TXT and .mat)

- Water velocity data files including:

  - Top surface velocity profiles (.top)

  - Channel bottom velocity profiles (.bot)

  - Average velocity profiles (.vav)

  - Total velocity profiles describing velocities at all depths (.vel)

- Detailed depth profiles (.wab)

- GPS-based transect paths taken by measuring crews (.kml)

Measurement summaries include field notes from measurement crews as well as summary data of each measurement. A typical field notes file, named "measurement.pdf" in the data archive, includes a "front sheet" indicating the conditions and parameters (date, time, weather conditions, equipment used, and other details) under which the measurement was made. This will be followed by any available measurement summaries showing the computed parameters of the measurement such as streamflow (discharge), cross section area, width, and average velocities. In many cases, flow rates were determined from transects that also were used for velocity mapping or bathymetric mapping. Viewers will note, in these cases, that the measurement transects are often a small subset of a larger number of transects that were used for mapping.

The measurement data files include all of the raw files (.PD0 and .riv) that were produced by the ADCP software, as well as summary files (.mmt and .wsp) that contain processing commands and settings unique to each measurement, generated when the operators processed and quality-checked these measurements. Users will need to be familiar with Teledyne RDI's® WinRiverII™ software to open the .PD0/ .mmt files or SonTek's® River Surveyor Live™ software to open the .riv/.wsp files.

Export files, which are useful as input files for further processing, have been placed within most data archive folders. The format of these files is defined by the vendors, and is intended to be importable to any number of software applications for further analysis. In particular, the _ASC.TXT files are a text format, whereas the .mat files are in a MatLab format (Mathworks, 2005). Each export file represents one

transect, which is a single pass across the measurement section in a direction perpendicular to the flow. Each transect file is organized into ensembles and bins as shown in figure 15. An ensemble is a column of water from the surface to the streambed whose width is the distance that the measuring boat travels in about 1 second (typically on the order of a few inches to a few feet). The ADCP records many ensembles as it crosses a river from one bank to the other, with ensembles getting taller as the depth increases and wider as boat speed increases. These ensembles are divided into depth bins, representing individual velocity measurements by the ADCP at different depths as shown in figure 15.

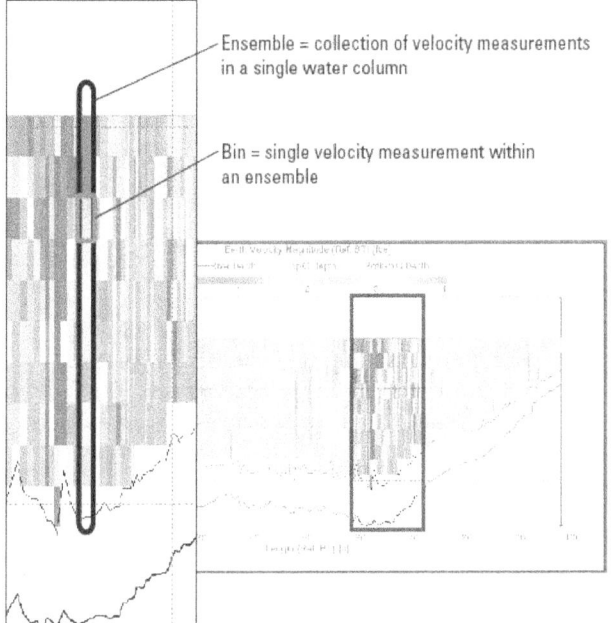

Figure 15. A typical acoustic Doppler current profiler measurement ensemble and bin.

Further processing was done for most measurements to create velocity and depth profiles. Published profiles include .top files, which describe the velocities in the first measured bin of each ensemble within each transect. Note that the first measured bin typically occurs between 1 and 4 feet below the water surface due to the draft of the instrument and a blanking distance directly beneath the transducer. There also are .bot files that list the velocities of the measured bins closest to the streambed within each transect. Like the top bins, bottom bins do not reach all the way to the intended surface, the streambed, because of side-lobe interference (Mueller and Wagner, 2009). Users can compare the .bot files to the .wab files (described later in this section) to understand how much distance is unmeasured at the bottom of each ensemble. Depth-averaged ensemble velocities are given in the .vav files; these files contain one velocity value for each column of water, averaged from the streambed to the surface. Detailed velocity profiles for all measured bins within the transect have been generated as .vel files. The four file types described above are in a text file format as tab-separated values. Locations listed in the files are given in meters based on the Universal Transverse Mercator (UTM) coordinate system, zone 16. The fields labeled "u" and "v" are used in the files to describe the east and north velocities, respectively, but velocity magnitude and direction also are reported in the "mag" and "hdir" fields, where "hdir" refers to horizontal azimuth from true north. All velocities are reported in feet per second. Elevation fields should be ignored in these four files because they are based on GPS data with low vertical accuracy, combined with arbitrary GPS antenna heights. The .wab files found in the data archive provide information about depths from the water surface to the streambed in meters, using the same UTM zone 16 coordinates as the velocity profiles, also in meters. Again, it is important to note that the elevation field in this and other profile files should be ignored because the placement of GPS antennas varied widely from measurement to measurement.

Users wishing to visualize the actual paths of each measurement transect will find kml ship track files within each measurement folder. Within the ship track file, transects are numbered from one to the total number of transects that were used in that measurement. Because multiple transects may have been aborted or unused in the measurement, the transect numbers will not necessarily match the transect numbers found in the measurement summaries. In some cases, the ship track files were not generated at all due to a lack of GPS data.

Summary

The U.S. Geological Survey initiated a substantial effort in the summer of 2011 to measure and document the record-setting floods of the Mississippi and Ohio Rivers. The activation of the New Madrid Floodway, which had not occurred since 1937, provided a unique opportunity to collect a dataset describing a flood wave downstream from a levee breach as well as the characteristics of flow through a large floodway. A total of 42 stage sensing devices collected time series of water levels within the floodway.

U.S. Geological Survey crews also conducted measurements of depth, velocity, and streamflow at selected locations in the floodway and the main channels of the Mississippi and Ohio Rivers throughout the period from late April to late June. The U.S. Geological Survey made more than 200 discrete observations of streamflow near the Ohio River and Mississippi River confluence, as well as inside and outside of the floodway. These measurements are summarized in this report and stored in a publicly available online data archive. These data provide both insight into the hydrodynamics of levee breaches and the hydrodynamics of large river/floodway interaction.

References Cited

Camillo, C.A., 2012, Divine providence—The 2011 flood in the Mississippi River and tributaries project: Vicksburg, Mississippi, Mississippi River Commission, 312 p.

Langbein, W.B., and Iseri, K.T., 1960, General introduction and hydrologic definitions: U.S. Geological Survey Water-Supply Paper 1541–A, 29 p.

Mason, R.R., Jr., and Weiger, B.A., 1995, Stream gaging and flood forecasting—A Partnership of the U.S. Geological Survey and the National Weather Service: U.S. Dept. of the Interior, U.S. Geological Survey: National Oceanic and Atmospheric Administration, U.S. Dept. of Commerce, accessed November 19, 2012, at *http://water.usgs.gov/wid/ FS_209-95/mason-weiger.html.*

Mathworks, Inc., 2005, Matlab—The language of technical computing: Natick, Massachusets, ver. 7.1.

McGee, B.D, Goree, B.B., Tollett, R.W., Woodward, B.K., and Kress, W.H., 2005, Hurricane Rita surge data, southwestern Louisiana and southeastern Texas, September to November 2005: U.S. Geological Survey Data Series Report 220, accessed March 21, 2013, at *http://pubs.usgs.gov/ ds/2006/220/.*

Mississippi River Commission, 2011, 2011 MR&T Flood Report: U.S. Army Corps of Engineers, 45 p., accessed March 21, 2013, at *http://www.mvd.usace.army.mil/ Portals/52/docs/MRC/MRC_2011_Flood_Report.pdf.*

Mississippi River Commision, 2012, The Mississippi River and Tributaries Project—Birds Point-New Madrid Floodway Information Paper: U.S. Army Corps of Engineers, 17 p., accessed March 21, 2013 at *http://www.mvd.usace. army.mil/Portals/52/docs/Birds%20Point-New%20 Madrid%20info%20paper%20FINAL%200426.pdf.*

Mueller, D.S., and Wagner, C.R., 2009, Measuring discharge with acoustic Doppler current profilers from a moving boat: U.S. Geological Survey Techniques and Methods, book 3, chap. A22, 72 p.

Rydlund, P.H., Jr., and Densmore, B.K., 2012, Methods of practice and guidelines for using survey-grade global navigation satellite systems (GNSS) to establish vertical datum in the United States Geological Survey: U.S. Geological Survey Techniques and Methods, book 11, chap. D1, 102 p. with appendixes.

U.S. Geological Survey, 2008, National Water Information System: U.S. Geological Survey Web interface, accessed on April 29, 2013, at *http://nwis.waterdata.usgs.gov.*

Glossary

Note: Glossary definitions are taken from Langbein and Iseri (1960) whenever possible.

discharge In its simplest concept discharge means outflow; therefore, the use of this term is not restricted as to course or location, and it can be applied to describe the flow of water from a pipe or from a drainage basin.

flood An overflow or inundation that comes from a river or other body of water, and causes or threatens damage.

flood peak The highest value of the stage or streamflow attained by a flood, often designated as peak stage or peak streamflow, respectively.

flood stage The stage at which overflow of the natural banks of a stream begins to cause damage in the reach where the water-surface elevation is measured.

hydrograph A graph showing stage, streamflow, velocity, or other property of water with respect to time.

peak stage See flood peak.

peak streamflow See flood peak.

precipitation As used in hydrology, precipitation is the discharge of water, in liquid or solid state, out of the atmosphere, generally upon a land or water surface. It is the common process by which atmospheric water becomes surface or subsurface water. The term "precipitation" also commonly is used to designate the quantity of water that is precipitated.

stage Height of a water surface above an established datum, also known as gage height.

streamflow Discharge from a natural channel. Although the term discharge can be applied to flow in a canal, the word streamflow uniquely describes the discharge in a surface stream course. The units of measurement often are reported in cubic feet per second (ft^3/s).

streamgage A particular site on a stream where a record of streamflow is obtained.

trend The change of a particular variable with either time or spatial location as computed by statistical analysis.

Table 4.   Streamflow measurements at stations near the New Madrid Floodway during the Midwest floods of 2011.

[Sources include: PD0: U.S. Geological Survey (USGS) measurements using TRDI WinRiverII™ platform; riv: USGS measurements using SonTek® RiverSurveyor™ platform; USACE: Measurements made by the U.S. Army Corps of Engineers. N, no; Y, yes]

Station number	Station name	Source	Additional files[a] available: Velocity	kml	Streamflow (cubic feet per second) Main channel	Overflow	Total
			April 26				
03611500	Ohio River at Metropolis, Illinois	PD0	N	N			1,080,000
			April 28				
07022000	Mississippi River at Thebes, Illinois	PD0	Y	Y			777,000
365730089063001	Mississippi River below Ohio confluence	PD0	Y	Y			1,830,000
			April 29				
07022000	Mississippi River at Thebes, Illinois	PD0	Y	Y			766,000
370000089122601	Mississippi River above Cairo, Illinois	PD0	Y	Y	660,000	176,000	836,000
365939089084601	Ohio River at Cairo, Illinois	PD0	Y	Y	800,000	172,000[b]	972,000
			April 30				
370000089122601	Mississippi River above Cairo, Illinois	PD0	Y	Y			836,000
365939089084601	Ohio River at Cairo, Illinois	PD0	Y	Y	778,000	181,000[b]	959,000
365730089063001	Mississippi River below Ohio confluence	PD0	Y	Y			1,830,000
			May 1				
370000089122601	Mississippi River above Cairo, Illinois	PD0	Y	Y			811,000
365939089084601	Ohio River at Cairo, Illinois	PD0	N	Y	854,000	205,000[b]	1,060,000
365730089063001	Mississippi River below Ohio confluence	PD0	Y	Y			1,870,000
			May 2				
370000089122601	Mississippi River above Cairo, Illinois	PD0	Y	Y	637,000	177,000	815,000
365939089084601	Ohio River at Cairo, Illinois	PD0	Y	Y	873,000	239,000[b]	1,110,000
			May 3				
03611500	Ohio River at Metropolis, Illinois	PD0	Y	N			1,300,000
07022000	Mississippi River at Thebes, Illinois	PD0	Y	Y			730,000
370000089122601	Mississippi River above Cairo, Illinois	PD0	N	Y	694,000	183,000[b]	877,000
365939089084601	Ohio River at Cairo, Illinois	PD0	Y	Y	999,000	270,000[b]	1,270,000
365659089073101	New Madrid Floodway upper inflow breach at Birds Point	PD0	Y	Y			404,000
365638089060600	Mississippi River below Birds Point levee	PD0	Y	Y			1,650,000
363454089285900	New Madrid Floodway lower breach no. 2	PD0	Y	Y			18,600
363524089302700	New Madrid Floodway outflow 1,500-foot gap	PD0	Y	Y			113,000
			May 4				
370000089122601	Mississippi River above Cairo, Illinois	PD0	Y	Y			833,000
365939089084601	Ohio River at Cairo, Illinois	PD0	Y	Y	997,000	293,000[riv]	1,290,000
365659089073101	New Madrid Floodway upper inflow breach at Birds Point	PD0	Y	Y			397,000
365659089073101	New Madrid Floodway upper inflow breach at Birds Point	riv	Y	Y			375,000
365638089060600	Mississippi River below Birds Point levee	PD0	Y	Y			1,610,000
363618089251701	New Madrid Floodway combined outflow	riv	Y	Y			313,000
			May 5				
370000089122601	Mississippi River above Cairo, Illinois	PD0	Y	Y			758,000

Table 4   25

Table 4. Streamflow measurements at stations near the New Madrid Floodway during the Midwest Floods of 2011.—Continued

[Sources include: PD0: U.S. Geological Survey (USGS) measurements using TRDI WinRiverII™ platform; riv: USGS measurements using SonTek® RiverSurveyor™ platform; USACE: Measurements made by the U.S. Army Corps of Engineers. N, no; Y, yes]

Station number	Station name	Source	Additional files[a] available:		Streamflow (cubic feet per second)		
			Velocity	kml	Main channel	Overflow	Total
365939089084601	Ohio River at Cairo, Illinois	PD0	Y	Y	1,020,000	285,000[b]	1,310,000
365659089073101	New Madrid Floodway upper inflow breach at Birds Point	riv	Y	Y			365,000
365638089060600	Mississippi River below Birds Point levee	PD0	Y	Y			1,700,000
362216089303901	Mississippi River at Tiptonville, Tennessee	PD0	Y	Y			2,040,000
	May 6						
370000089122601	Mississippi River above Cairo, Illinois	PD0	Y	Y			689,000
365939089084601	Ohio River at Cairo, Illinois	PD0	Y	Y	1,060,000	285,000[b]	1,350,000
365659089073101	New Madrid Floodway upper inflow breach at Birds Point	riv	Y	Y			352,000
365659089073101	New Madrid Floodway upper inflow breach at Birds Point	PD0	Y	Y			382,000
365638089060600	Mississippi River below Birds Point levee	PD0	Y	Y			1,580,000
363740089180601	New Madrid Floodway middle breach no. 1	PD0	Y	Y			4,440
363618089251701	New Madrid Floodway combined outflow	PD0	N	Y			383,000
	May 7						
365659089073101	New Madrid Floodway upper inflow breach at Birds Point	PD0	Y	Y			380,000
363618089251701	New Madrid Floodway combined outflow	PD0	N	Y			377,000
	May 8						
370000089122601	Mississippi River above Cairo, Illinois	PD0	N	Y	537,000	84,000[b]	621,000
365939089084601	Ohio River at Cairo, Illinois	PD0	N	Y	1,070,000	281,000[b]	1,350,000
365659089073101	New Madrid Floodway upper inflow breach at Birds Point	PD0	Y	Y			347,000
07024070	Mississippi River at Hickman, Kentucky	USACE	N	N			1,675,000
363740089180601	New Madrid Floodway middle breach no. 1	PD0	Y	Y			15,400
363618089251701	New Madrid Floodway combined outflow	PD0	Y	Y			362,000
362216089303901	Mississippi River at Tiptonville, Tennessee	USACE	N	N			1,942,000
	May 9						
370000089122601	Mississippi River above Cairo, Illinois	PD0	Y	Y			582,000
365939089084601	Ohio River at Cairo, Illinois	PD0	Y	Y	1,000,000	274,000[b]	1,270,000
365659089073101	New Madrid Floodway upper inflow breach at Birds Point	PD0	N	Y			307,000
07024070	Mississippi River at Hickman, Ky	USACE	N	N			1,625,000
363740089180601	New Madrid Floodway middle breach no. 1	PD0	Y	Y			18,200
363618089251701	New Madrid Floodway combined outflow	PD0	Y	Y			349,000
362216089303901	Mississippi River at Tiptonville, Tennessee	USACE	N	N			1,943,000
	May 10						
07022000	Mississippi River at Thebes, Illinois	PD0	Y	Y			551,000
370000089122601	Mississippi River above Cairo, Illinois	PD0	Y	Y			559,000

Table 4.   Streamflow measurements at stations near the New Madrid Floodway during the Midwest Floods of 2011.—Continued

[Sources include: PD0: U.S. Geological Survey (USGS) measurements using TRDI WinRiverII™ platform; riv: USGS measurements using SonTek® RiverSurveyor™ platform; USACE: Measurements made by the U.S. Army Corps of Engineers. N, no; Y, yes]

Station number	Station name	Source	Additional files[a] available:		Streamflow (cubic feet per second)		
			Velocity	kml	Main channel	Overflow	Total
365659089073101	New Madrid Floodway upper inflow breach at Birds Point	PD0	Y	Y			271,000
07024070	Mississippi River at Hickman, Kentucky	USACE	N	N			1,605,000
363740089180601	New Madrid Floodway middle breach no. 1	riv	Y	Y			23,500
363618089251701	New Madrid Floodway combined outflow	riv	Y	Y			342,000
362216089303901	Mississippi River at Tiptonville, Tennessee	USACE	N	N			1,895,000
	May 11						
370000089122601	Mississippi River above Cairo, Illinois	PD0	Y	Y			526,000
365939089084601	Ohio River at Cairo, Illinois	PD0	Y	Y	997,000	255,000[b]	1,250,000
365939089084601	Ohio River at Cairo, Illinois	PD0	Y	Y	1,020,000	255,000[b]	1,280,000
365659089073101	New Madrid Floodway upper inflow breach at Birds Point	PD0	Y	Y			281,000
07024070	Mississippi River at Hickman, Kentucky	USACE	N	N			1,575,000
363740089180601	New Madrid Floodway middle breach no. 1	PD0	Y	Y			20,800
363618089251701	New Madrid Floodway combined outflow	PD0	Y	Y			334,000
362216089303901	Mississippi River at Tiptonville, Tennessee	USACE	N	N			1,875,000
	May 12						
370000089122601	Mississippi River above Cairo, Illinois	PD0	Y	Y			546,000
365939089084601	Ohio River at Cairo, Illinois	PD0	Y	Y	966,000	251,000	1,220,000
365659089073101	New Madrid Floodway upper inflow breach at Birds Point	PD0	Y	Y			254,000
07024070	Mississippi River at Hickman, Kentucky	USACE	N	N			1,555,000
363740089180601	New Madrid Floodway middle breach no. 1	PD0	Y	Y			61,300
363618089251701	New Madrid Floodway combined outflow	PD0	Y	Y			324,000
362216089303901	Mississippi River at Tiptonville, Tennessee	USACE	N	N			1,858,000
	May 13						
365659089073101	New Madrid Floodway upper inflow breach at Birds Point	PD0	Y	Y			221,000
363740089180601	New Madrid Floodway middle breach no. 1	PD0	Y	Y			75,600
363618089251701	New Madrid Floodway combined outflow	PD0	Y	Y			330,000
	May 14						
370000089122601	Mississippi River above Cairo, Illinois	PD0	Y	Y			519,000
365939089084601	Ohio River at Cairo, Illinois	PD0	Y	Y	964,000	205,000[b]	1,170,000
365659089073101	New Madrid Floodway upper inflow breach at Birds Point	PD0	Y	Y			198,000
365638089060600	Mississippi River below Birds Point levee	PD0	Y	Y			1,390,000
07024070	Mississippi River At Hickman, Kentucky	USACE	N	N			1,430,000
363740089180601	New Madrid Floodway middle breach no. 1	PD0	Y	Y			82,500

Table 4   27

Table 4. Streamflow measurements at stations near the New Madrid Floodway during the Midwest Floods of 2011.—Continued

[Sources include: PD0: U.S. Geological Survey (USGS) measurements using TRDI WinRiverII™ platform; riv: USGS measurements using SonTek® RiverSurveyor™ platform; USACE: Measurements made by the U.S. Army Corps of Engineers. N, no; Y, yes]

Station number	Station name	Source	Additional files[a] available: Velocity	kml	Streamflow (cubic feet per second) Main channel	Overflow	Total
363618089251701	New Madrid Floodway combined outflow	PD0	Y	Y			314,000
362216089303901	Mississippi River at Tiptonville, Tennessee	USACE	N	N	1,604,000	98,000	1,702,000
				May 15			
370000089122601	Mississippi River above Cairo, Illinois	PD0	Y	Y			509,000
365939089084601	Ohio River at Cairo, Illinois	PD0	Y	Y	900,000	181,000	1,080,000
365659089073101	New Madrid Floodway upper inflow breach at Birds Point	PD0	N	Y			159,000
07024070	Mississippi River At Hickman, Kentucky	USACE	N	N			1,391,000
363740089180601	New Madrid Floodway middle breach no. 1	PD0	Y	Y			86,300
363618089251701	New Madrid Floodway combined outflow	PD0	N	Y			288,000
362216089303901	Mississippi River at Tiptonville, Tennessee	USACE	N	N	1,544,000	82,000	1,626,000
				May 16			
370000089122601	Mississippi River above Cairo, Illinois	PD0	N	Y			507,000
365939089084601	Ohio River at Cairo, Illinois	PD0	Y	Y	886,000	155,000	1,040,000
365659089073101	New Madrid Floodway upper inflow breach at Birds Point	PD0	N	N			128,000
365638089060600	Mississippi River below Birds Point levee	PD0	Y	Y			1,340,000
07024070	Mississippi River At Hickman, Kentucky	USACE	N	N			1,379,000
363740089180601	New Madrid Floodway middle breach no. 1	PD0	Y	Y			87,100
363618089251701	New Madrid Floodway combined outflow	PD0	N	Y			264,000
362216089303901	Mississippi River at Tiptonville, Tennessee	USACE	N	N	1,522,000	72,000	1,594,000
				May 17			
03611500	Ohio River at Metropolis, Illinois	PD0	N	N			931,000
370000089122601	Mississippi River above Cairo, Illinois	PD0	N	Y			507,000
365939089084601	Ohio River at Cairo, Illinois	PD0	Y	Y	807,000	145,000[b]	952,000
365659089073101	New Madrid Floodway upper inflow breach at Birds Point	PD0	N	N			101,000
07024070	Mississippi River at Hickman, Kentucky	USACE	N	N			1,355,000
363740089180601	New Madrid Floodway middle breach no. 1	PD0	Y	Y			86,900
363618089251701	New Madrid Floodway combined outflow	PD0	N	Y			241,000
362216089303901	Mississippi River at Tiptonville, Tennessee	USACE	N	N	1,493,000	66,000	1,559,000
				May 18			
370000089122601	Mississippi River above Cairo, Illinois	PD0	Y	Y	464,000	43,600[b]	508,000
365939089084601	Ohio River at Cairo, Illinois	PD0	Y	Y	763,000	101,000	864,000
365659089073101	New Madrid Floodway upper inflow breach at Birds Point	riv	Y	Y			71,200
07024070	Mississippi River at Hickman, Kentucky	USACE	N	N			1,305,000
363740089180601	New Madrid Floodway middle breach no. 1	PD0	Y	Y			83,700
363618089251701	New Madrid Floodway combined outflow	PD0	N	Y			210,000

Table 4. Streamflow measurements at stations near the New Madrid Floodway during the Midwest Floods of 2011.—Continued

[Sources include: PD0: U.S. Geological Survey (USGS) measurements using TRDI WinRiverII™ platform; riv: USGS measurements using SonTek® RiverSurveyor™ platform; USACE: Measurements made by the U.S. Army Corps of Engineers. N, no; Y, yes]

Station number	Station name	Source	Additional files[a] available:		Streamflow (cubic feet per second)		
			Velocity	kml	Main channel	Overflow	Total
362216089303901	Mississippi River at Tiptonville, Tennessee	USACE	N	N	1,480,000	47,000	1,527,000
May 19							
365659089073101	New Madrid Floodway upper inflow breach at Birds Point	riv	N	N			61,100
365659089073101	New Madrid Floodway upper inflow breach at Birds Point	PD0	Y	Y			61,000
07024070	Mississippi River at Hickman, Kentucky	USACE	N	N			1,243,000
363740089180601	New Madrid Floodway middle breach no. 1	PD0	Y	Y			76,700
363618089251701	New Madrid Floodway combined outflow	PD0	N	Y			183,000
May 20							
370000089122601	Mississippi River above Cairo, Illinois	riv	Y	Y			483,000
365939089084601	Ohio River at Cairo, Illinois	PD0	Y	Y	671,000	86,800	758,000
365659089073101	New Madrid Floodway upper inflow breach at Birds Point	PD0	Y	Y			27,900
365638089060600	Mississippi River below Birds Point levee	PD0	Y	Y			1,240,000
363740089180601	New Madrid Floodway middle breach no. 1	PD0	Y	Y			63,000
363618089251701	New Madrid Floodway combined outflow	PD0	N	Y			147,000
May 21							
370000089122601	Mississippi River above Cairo, Illinois	PD0	Y	Y	465,000	21,200[b]	486,000
365939089084601	Ohio River at Cairo, Illinois	PD0	Y	Y	642,000	60,800	703,000
365659089073101	New Madrid Floodway upper inflow breach at Birds Point	riv	Y	Y			15,800
365638089060600	Mississippi River below Birds Point levee	PD0	Y	Y			1,170,000
363740089180601	New Madrid Floodway middle breach no. 1	riv	Y	Y			50,700
363618089251701	New Madrid Floodway combined outflow	PD0	N	Y			127,000
May 22							
370000089122601	Mississippi River above Cairo, Illinois	PD0	Y	Y	467,000	14,100[b]	481,000
365939089084601	Ohio River at Cairo, Illinois	PD0	Y	Y	592,000	46,100	638,000
365638089060600	Mississippi River below Birds Point levee	PD0	Y	Y			1,100,000
363740089180601	New Madrid Floodway middle breach no. 1	riv	Y	Y			40,100
363618089251701	New Madrid Floodway combined outflow	riv	N	N			87,000
May 23							
370000089122601	Mississippi River above Cairo, Illinois	PD0	Y	Y	469,000	7,050[b]	476,000
365939089084601	Ohio River at Cairo, Illinois	PD0	Y	Y	585,000	36,000	621,000
365638089060600	Mississippi River below Birds Point levee	PD0	Y	Y			1,100,000
363618089251701	New Madrid Floodway combined outflow	riv	Y	Y			75,500
May 24							
370000089122601	Mississippi River above Cairo, Illinois	PD0	Y	Y			491,000
365939089084601	Ohio River at Cairo, Illinois	PD0	Y	Y	561,000	29,500	591,000

Table 4   29

Table 4. Streamflow measurements at stations near the New Madrid Floodway during the Midwest Floods of 2011.—Continued

[Sources include: PD0: U.S. Geological Survey (USGS) measurements using TRDI WinRiverII™ platform; riv: USGS measurements using SonTek® RiverSurveyor™ platform; USACE: Measurements made by the U.S. Army Corps of Engineers. N, no; Y, yes]

Station number	Station name	Source	Additional files[a] available:		Streamflow (cubic feet per second)		
			Velocity	kml	Main channel	Overflow	Total
365659089073101	New Madrid Floodway upper inflow breach at Birds Point	riv	Y	Y			3,550
363740089180601	New Madrid Floodway middle breach no. 1	riv	Y	Y			28,900
363618089251701	New Madrid Floodway combined outflow	riv	Y	Y			54,000
	May 25						
365659089073101	New Madrid Floodway upper inflow breach at Birds Point	riv	Y	Y			1,110
363618089251701	New Madrid Floodway combined outflow	riv	Y	Y			45,400
	May 26						
365659089073101	New Madrid Floodway upper inflow breach at Birds Point	riv	Y	Y			738
363740089180601	New Madrid Floodway middle breach no. 1	riv	Y	Y			19,300
363618089251701	New Madrid Floodway combined outflow	riv	Y	Y			35,100
	May 27						
365659089073101	New Madrid Floodway upper inflow breach at Birds Point	riv	Y	Y			695
363740089180601	New Madrid Floodway middle breach no. 1	riv	Y	Y			13,600
363618089251701	New Madrid Floodway combined outflow	riv	Y	Y			29,000
	May 28						
365659089073101	New Madrid Floodway upper inflow breach at Birds Point	riv	Y	Y			461
363740089180601	New Madrid Floodway middle breach no. 1	riv	Y	Y			12,900
363618089251701	New Madrid Floodway combined outflow	riv	Y	Y			28,100
	May 29						
365659089073101	New Madrid Floodway upper inflow breach at Birds Point	riv	Y	Y			647
363740089180601	New Madrid Floodway middle breach no. 1	riv	Y	Y			12,100
	May 30						
365659089073101	New Madrid Floodway upper inflow breach at Birds Point	riv	Y	Y			730
363740089180601	New Madrid Floodway middle breach no. 1	riv	Y	Y			13,500
363454089285900	New Madrid Floodway lower breach no. 2	riv	N	N			706
363524089302700	New Madrid Floodway outflow 1,500-foot gap	riv	Y	Y			22,400
	May 31						
03611500	Ohio River at Metropolis, Illinois	PD0	N	N			553,000
365659089073101	New Madrid Floodway upper inflow breach at Birds Point	riv	Y	Y			1,700

Table 4. Streamflow measurements at stations near the New Madrid Floodway during the Midwest Floods of 2011.—Continued

[Sources include: PD0: U.S. Geological Survey (USGS) measurements using TRDI WinRiverII™ platform; riv: USGS measurements using SonTek® RiverSurveyor™ platform; USACE: Measurements made by the U.S. Army Corps of Engineers. N, no; Y, yes]

Station number	Station name	Source	Additional files[a] available:		Streamflow (cubic feet per second)		
			Velocity	kml	Main channel	Overflow	Total
363740089180601	New Madrid Floodway middle breach no. 1	riv	Y	Y			15,600
363454089285900	New Madrid Floodway lower breach no. 2	riv	Y	Y			662
363524089302700	New Madrid Floodway outflow 1,500-foot gap	riv	Y	Y			21,900
	June 1						
365659089073101	New Madrid Floodway upper inflow breach at Birds Point	riv	Y	Y			1,760
363740089180601	New Madrid Floodway middle breach no. 1	riv	Y	Y			16,300
363454089285900	New Madrid Floodway lower breach no. 2	riv	Y	Y			649
363524089302700	New Madrid Floodway outflow 1,500-foot gap	riv	Y	Y			21,200
	June 2						
365659089073101	New Madrid Floodway upper inflow breach at Birds Point	riv	Y	Y			916
363740089180601	New Madrid Floodway middle breach no. 1	riv	Y	Y			15,300
363454089285900	New Madrid Floodway lower breach no. 2	riv	Y	Y			696
363524089302700	New Madrid Floodway outflow 1,500-foot gap	riv	Y	Y			20,800
	June 3						
365659089073101	New Madrid Floodway upper inflow breach at Birds Point	riv	Y	Y			no inflow
363740089180601	New Madrid Floodway middle breach no. 1	riv	Y	Y			12,900
363454089285900	New Madrid Floodway lower breach no. 2	riv	Y	Y			633
363524089302700	New Madrid Floodway outflow 1,500-foot gap	riv	Y	Y			21,600
	June 4						
365659089073101	New Madrid Floodway upper inflow breach at Birds Point	riv	Y	Y			no inflow
363740089180601	New Madrid Floodway middle breach no. 1	riv	Y	Y			7,160
363454089285900	New Madrid Floodway lower breach no. 2	riv	Y	Y			557
363524089302700	New Madrid Floodway outflow 1,500-foot gap	riv	Y	Y			20,900

Table 4   31

Table 4.   Streamflow measurements at stations near the New Madrid Floodway during the Midwest Floods of 2011.—Continued

[Sources include: PD0: U.S. Geological Survey (USGS) measurements using TRDI WinRiverII™ platform; riv: USGS measurements using SonTek® RiverSurveyor™ platform; USACE: Measurements made by the U.S. Army Corps of Engineers. N, no; Y, yes]

Station number	Station name	Source	Additional files[a] available:		Streamflow (cubic feet per second)		
			Velocity	kml	Main channel	Overflow	Total
June 5							
365659089073101	New Madrid Floodway upper inflow breach at Birds Point	riv	Y	Y			no inflow
363740089180601	New Madrid Floodway middle breach no. 1	riv	Y	Y			3,630
363454089285900	New Madrid Floodway lower breach no. 2	riv	Y	Y			357
363524089302700	New Madrid Floodway outflow 1,500-foot gap	riv	Y	Y			17,800
June 6							
363740089180601	New Madrid Floodway middle breach no. 1	riv	Y	Y			1,780
363618089251701	New Madrid Floodway combined outflow	riv	Y	Y			10,300
June 7							
07022000	Mississippi River at Thebes, Illinois	PD0	Y	Y			579,000
363740089180601	New Madrid Floodway middle breach no. 1	riv	Y	Y			413
363618089251701	New Madrid Floodway combined outflow	riv	N	N			9,590
June 8							
363618089251701	New Madrid Floodway combined outflow	riv	N	N			8,310
June 9							
363618089251701	New Madrid Floodway combined outflow	riv	N	N			6,880
June 10							
363618089251701	New Madrid Floodway combined outflow	riv	N	N			5,630
June 11							
363618089251701	New Madrid Floodway combined outflow	PD0	Y	Y			5,190
363618089251701	New Madrid Floodway combined outflow	riv	Y	Y			5,160
June 12							
363618089251701	New Madrid Floodway combined outflow	PD0	N	N			4,740
363618089251701	New Madrid Floodway combined outflow	riv	Y	Y			4,700
June 13							
363618089251701	New Madrid Floodway combined outflow	riv	Y	Y			4,190
June 14							
363618089251701	New Madrid Floodway combined outflow	riv	Y	Y			3,540

[a] Additional velocity files may include top, bottom, average, and total depth velocity profiles.

[b] Estimated.